Tower Hill

The First Twenty-five Years

The Entry Garden at Tower Hill

Tower Hill
The First Twenty-five Years

SELECTIVE MEMORIES OF A BENIGN DICTATOR

John W. Trexler

TidePool Press
Cambridge, Massachusetts

Copyright © 2017 by John Trexler

Published in the United States in 2017 by TidePool Press

All rights reserved.
No part of this book may be reproduced in any manner whatsoever without written permission.

Unless otherwise noted, the photos in this book are reproduced courtesy of the Collections of Tower Hill Botanic Garden, Boylston, MA, and the private collection of John Trexler and Robert Zeleniak.

TidePool Press
6 Maple Avenue, Cambridge, Massachusetts 02139
www.tidepoolpress.com

Printed in the United States

Library of Congress Cataloging-in-Publication Data

Trexler, John 1951-
    Tower Hill: The First Twenty-five Years, Selective Memories of a Benign Dictator
  p.cm.
  ISBN 978-0-9978482-0-5
  1. Trexler, John, Westborough, Massachusetts—United States—Biography
  2. Memoir 3. Tower Hill Botanic Garden—Boylston, Massachusetts
  4. Horticulture—Gardening 5. Master Planning 6. Public Gardens
  I. Title.

2017938921

WITH APPRECIATION

Robert Zeleniak
Trex and Emily
Philip Coen
Thomas Buchter
Clarence McKenzie Lewis
Marco Polo Stufano
Norma Mortenson

IN RECOGNITION OF

The Worcester County Horticultural Society
on the occasion of its 175th Anniversary

John leading a tour of the Lawn Garden, 1988

———— CONTENTS ————

Foreword		IX
Chapter One	California Story	1
Chapter Two	Mosquitos, Stock, Lilac and Ancient Rome	9
Chapter Three	Taking Root	15
Chapter Four	Right Place, Right Time	33
Chapter Five	From the Inside Out	61
Chapter Six	A Garden of People	121
Chapter Seven	Honor Roll	143
Chapter Eight	A Garden within Reach	169
Conclusion	Festina Lente	193
Appendix		197
Acknowledgments		219

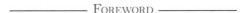

Foreword

IN AN AGE that worships creative disruption and entrepreneurial imagination, surprisingly little attention is given to the practice and virtues of reinvigorating venerable institutions. Sustaining older institutions and keeping them fit, relevant and forward-looking in a fast changing landscape offers social continuity and the communal benefit of prudent risk-taking and social change. Worcester, Massachusetts—New England's second largest city—is something of an exemplar as a number of the city's pre-eminent cultural and civic institutions, whose origins were in the nineteenth century, remain leaders in their respective fields today. Examples include the American Antiquarian Society (1812), the Children's Friend (Worcester Children's Friend Society 1849), the Ecotarium (Worcester Natural History Society 1884), the Worcester Historical Museum (Worcester Society of Antiquity 1875) and the Worcester Art Museum (1898). As progressive as each of these institutions has been and continues to be, it would be hard to match the transformational resilience of the Worcester County Horticultural Society (WCHS) which was founded in 1842—with roots in the Worcester Agricultural Society (1819). Relocated in 1986 from downtown Worcester to a magnificent site twelve miles away in the countryside of Boylston and officially retaining its original name, WCHS is now far better known as Tower Hill Botanic Garden. John Trexler, the animating spirit who led the transformation, has written an account that is fascinating in its own right, but which may inspire others to take a fresh look at the untapped vitality tucked away in older institutions.

Constructive institutional change is never easy. It takes vision, persuasiveness, support from diverse quarters, persistence and more than a little of what might be called romantic pragmatism. Above all it takes leadership, a "benign dictator" as John Trexler refers to himself in the title of this wonderful memoir. Horticulture can be ephemeral in the particular—a flower's prime bloom is lovely but momentary—but when considered as a system, as a botanic garden, then horizons shift from weeks to decades and well beyond. Writing about gardens a century ago, Alice Morse Earle, a Worcester native and historian of early America, said, "Half the interest of a garden is the constant exercise of the imagination ... to be content with the present and not striving about the future is fatal." A lover of plants and gardens, John Trexler reveled in their presence from an early age, but his distinguishing gifts have been his ability to imagine the future and his vigilance in bringing that vision to life.

John's arrival in Worcester in 1984 as the new Executive Director of WCHS was inauspicious. His immediate predecessor, Fred Roberts, had served for less than half a year before moving on to what would become a distinguished twenty-two year career as director of Pierre S. du Pont's Longwood Gardens in Kennett Square. When John arrived in Worcester—inadvertently on a holiday—the Society had just two other employees, an outmoded facility in downtown Worcester, thoughts of moving outside the city, and no chairman of the board. John used the holiday to read through nearly one hundred and fifty years of the Society's annual reports. Even if the future looked bleak, the history was intriguing.

Formally established in 1842, WCHS had its origins in the Worcester Agricultural Society which had been founded in 1819 to promote not only agriculture and livestock, but local manufacture as well. The Agricultural Society became a victim of its own success as its annual cattle show was a social high point of the year and its horse races attracted betting and public drinking, which detracted from its higher minded original goals of education and the promotion of local products. The founding of WCHS—interestingly, initiated and sustained by more than a few leaders of the Worcester Agricultural Society—was a testament to Worcester's nascent emergence as a steam, rather than

Foreword

water-powered, manufacturing center. Commercial prosperity in finance, manufacturing and trade was surpassing agriculture in the county. As was already evident in England and to a lesser extent through much of coastal America, gardening was superceding farming as a community pursuit. And one need not be rich to garden. Writing in 1936, Albert Farnsworth called the period from 1830-1860 as the "Golden Age" of gardening in Worcester, a period when he noted "everybody had a garden." That might be a contestable claim, but it certainly made the 1842 WCHS mission of "advancing the science and encouraging and improving the practice of horticulture" both timely and popular.

Worcester County has a long agricultural tradition, even if it lacks an agricultural identity relative to, say, the Pioneer Valley or the South Coast in Massachusetts or the Hudson Valley in New York. The recent USDA census of direct farm to consumer sales by county offers the surprising fact that Worcester County ranks sixth in the United States in total dollar volume. Sweet corn, tomatoes and lettuce play a role, but it's really due to the diversity of products grown. Orchards and nurseries throughout Worcester County combine with farm stands to create a remarkably robust, if under-recognized, horticultural region.

What does all this have to do with John Trexler and this wonderful memoir? The timing of John's 1984 arrival on Elm Street in Worcester was more propitious than anyone could have appreciated at the time. Ever since the founding of WCHS, birthed as it was out of the Worcester Agricultural Society, there had been a natural and unresolved tension between the city and the surrounding hinterland. Worcester and other smaller county towns like Southbridge, Fitchburg, Whitinsville, Athol, Clinton, Ware, Gardner and Leominster had sustained exposure in the industrial sun. The hinterlands slipped into the shadows as cities and towns became increasingly dependent on the industrialized food chain which sourced products from all over the world at increasingly low cost, especially after World War II. While WCHS never lost interest in supporting farmers and orchardists, the emphasis had shifted over the years toward flowers and ornamental trees. The high point of the WCHS year was the annual flower show, an ambitious and socially popular production held at the organization's 30 Elm Street headquarters in downtown Worcester. Popular as it was, the show was an energetic spike in a generally flat year and WCHS was at something of a crossroads. When John arrived, the board was considering one of three options: maintain the status quo; merge with a compatible organization or; as improbably ambitious as it must have sounded, "develop a horticulture center in an accessible location." The rest, as they say, is history.

Only thirty-two in 1984, John promoted the bolder and far more adventurous path of moving WCHS out of Worcester and establishing Tower Hill Botanic Garden in Boylston. Clearly, he was a shrewdly enlightened, not just a "benign," dictator. He had the good sense and imagination to engage and, herein, generously credit a diverse cast of supporters—loyal staff, national experts, local philanthropists—to help him create what has become one of the most appealing horticultural institutions in the Northeast. Alexander Pope famously advised the Earl of Burlington on gardens for his newly built Chiswick House to "Consult the genius of the place." John did just that, not only with his plans for the remarkable Boylston property with its majestic view of Mt. Wachusett, but also through his deft engagement of people and institutions throughout Worcester County itself and beyond. Thanks to John's leadership, attentiveness to detail and overall vision, WCHS did not so much leave Worcester as it helped reconnect the second largest city in New England with its ecologically essential and aesthetically inspiring countryside.

In doing so, he used fifty years as his planning horizon—a remarkable perspective for a youthful activist. John Trexler's accomplishments in developing Tower Hill bring to mind an observation made in 1876 by another local horticultural luminary, Edward Winslow Lincoln, who, with his cousin Stephen Salisbury III, developed the Worcester park system: "It is given unto men to see visions and to dream dreams; yet it is vouchsafed to few to behold their realization."

Tower Hill: The First Twenty-Five Years is a wonderful account of a dream realized—an account that will appeal to anyone who visits Tower Hill, but even more importantly, a story that should inspire anyone with

Foreword

the imagination and commitment to re-invigorate and make current a venerable institution at an existential crossroad.

>Jock Herron
>Instructor in Architecture
>Collaborative Design Engineering
>Harvard Graduate School of Design
>Cambridge, MA

Tower Hill
The First Twenty-five Years

Oh, life is a glorious cycle of song,
A medley of extemporanea;
And love is a thing that can never go wrong;
And I am Marie of Romania.

—Dorothy Parker, *Not So Deep as a Well* (1937)

---- CHAPTER ONE ----

CALIFORNIA STORY

MY FATHER WAS a naval officer. We moved fifteen times by the time I was seventeen. Many of those moves involved long car rides imprisoned in the back seat with my three siblings. As the car sped along, I remember gazing out the window wondering what that blur of green was. At some point I learned that the green was trees—east coast trees, mid-west trees, mountain trees, west coast trees. I became determined to learn what each individual tree was. Thus began my long romance with gardening.

For forty-one years I worked in public horticulture. Seven years at Ringwood State Park, six years at the Morris County Park Commission—both in new Jersey, and twenty-eight years at the Worcester County Horticultural Society in Massachusetts. Those years were spent learning, gardening, guiding, teaching, designing, raising money and initiating and completing dozens of garden projects. I enjoyed every minute of every day. There were frustrations and setbacks but they were overshadowed by the many successes. This book is my story: from my gradual introduction to the world of gardening to the opportunity to build one of America's great public gardens, 1956-2012.

Above: Tulip tree (*Liriodendron tulipifera*)

Early in my career at the Worcester County Horticultural Society, Isabel Arms, Vice President of the Board of Trustees, reviewed my accomplishments and said, "These many realized goals are the work of a benign dictator, a man with a kindly and gracious disposition." I took this as a great compliment. Isabel would later make a bequest of more than a million dollars to the Society.

—⚘—

My very first plant memories are from when I was five years old living in a suburb of Madison, Wisconsin. Our house was part of a new development built on what had been farm fields and the old farmhouse was diagonally across the street. The couple that had farmed the land continued to maintain a large fruit and vegetable garden. I remember one solo visit to that garden where the farmer's wife let me pick currants. I had no concept of why or how this fruit came to be, but I do remember how good it tasted and how pleased my mother was to get a small bowl of the berries.

Kindergarten was not my "finest hour." If one could fail kindergarten I managed to do it. My one happy memory from that difficult year was the lesson of sowing a lima bean in a milk carton. One day we were told to bring an empty milk carton from the cafeteria after lunch. We were shown how to put soil into the carton, place a large bean seed into the soil and then add a bit of water. We wrote our names on the cartons and placed them on the windowsill. Each day we dutifully repeated the exercise of adding a small amount of water to the soil. When we returned to the classroom after the following weekend we witnessed with surprise and delight the emerging plants. The experience was simple, but, as it turned out, inspiring.

Not Even Asking

As an adult I gained a reputation for acquiring things for whichever institution I was working for. The first thing I ever acquired, however, was for myself, though it was unintentional. I was six years old. I had an

The Trexler family, 1955
Left to right: *Jimmy, Sally, John, Emily, Trex, Bobby*

earache. My father tried to relieve my discomfort by blowing cigarette smoke into my ear. It did not work. My mother's remedy was to put cotton in my ear—a lot of cotton. It did not work. They called a doctor who lived across the street and asked if he would take a quick look. "Sure" he said, "bring him over." I remember how young the doctor and his wife looked. They had me lie on my side on their kitchen table so they could get a good view of my ear. My gaze from that position was to the top of the refrigerator. There, I focused intently on a blue and red plastic wishing well. With his wife holding my head, the doctor slowly removed a wad of bloody cotton with tweezers. He examined the inside of my ear and finding no damage, gave me ear drops that immediately soothed the ache. During the procedure the wife had noticed me staring at the wishing well and, when I was ready to go home, she asked if I would like to have it. I didn't really want it, but I said yes to please them. A repaired ear and a toy—quite a night.

That was the first time I realized I had the ability to acquire things without really asking.

—⚋—

I was eight-years-old and living in Coronado, California, when I was introduced to what a "garden" is and the different aspects of gardening. At that age you tend to be fairly active—bike riding, roller-skating, skateboarding, and using our favorite toy the Flexible Flyer (the California version with wheels). We made a lot of noise and had a good time horsing around but there were times I needed a little eight-year-old quiet reflection. These moments led me to Dr. Wheeler's house next door. Dr. Wheeler had made it clear that no one—especially children—were to set foot in his yard. I was mesmerized by the beauty of his property and would stand on the sidewalk with the tips of my toes touching the edge of his perfect lawn, craning my neck to see what was inside the yard. I repeated this exercise on a regular basis. I'm sure Dr. Wheeler observed this weird little kid on more than one occasion. One day he appeared, introduced himself, and invited me into his yard. He asked me if I wanted to see his garden. This was my first memory of the term *garden*. What I remember is a lawn, green and soft under my bare feet, a fish pond and fountain with multi-colored fish, and a remarkable collection of orchids—what I now think were Cataleyas. This first adventure into a garden remains vivid. Shortly after my private tour of Dr. Wheeler's paradise, some neighborhood kids, under the cover of darkness, poisoned all the beautiful fish.

Prejudice and Genocide

About the time I had my adventure in Dr. Wheeler's garden, I was introduced to certain principles of gardening by my father. He had decided to replace all our grass with a popular grass substitute, Dichondra. He taught me the repetitive job of removing plugs of grass with an empty coffee can and replacing them with plugs of Dichondra. He hoped the ground cover would grow and eventually overwhelm the grass. It was one thing to slowly eradicate the grass; it was another more challenging chore to eliminate dandelions and other broad-leaved weeds that infiltrated the lawn. My father introduced me to a handy device called the "Killer Kane," a three-foot hollow plastic tube with a dispenser-nozzle at the bottom. You filled the transparent tube with water and then deposited a green tablet that reacted like a fizzy soft drink disk. The result was a reservoir of perfectly balanced liquid weed killer. My job was to methodically place the nozzle over the center of each weed, dowse the weed with the poison, and repeat the action until all the weeds were treated. The lesson was this: that there are certain plants so detestable and harmful to perfect harmony that they should be eliminated from the planet. Without realizing it, my father introduced me to two all too human traits: prejudice and genocide.

Propagation

Out of nowhere, or so it seems, I became obsessed with jade plant (*Crassula argentea*) and red geraniums (*Pelargonium x hortorum*). Dr. Wheeler taught me how to propagate these two plants. The technique

The Roman Forum from Encyclopedia Britannica

involved putting sandy soil into a clay pot, cutting off a tip of the "parent" plant, sticking it in the soil and waiting patiently for the plant to grow. Obtaining the soil was easy; the pots required a bike ride to the local hardware store and buying, with my allowance, six-inch clay pots. I arranged the pots on a terrace located outside my bedroom. They grew and flowered beautifully.

OTHER CHARACTER BUILDING LESSONS

My parents celebrated my birth by buying a TV. I grew up watching *Howdy Doody, Captain Kangaroo* and classic movies. I remember being spellbound by *Titanic*, starring Barbara Stanwyck and Clifton Webb. I had never heard of this great ship and I was not aware of its fate. The elegant interiors were captivating. You learn that, although the ship was touted as being "unsinkable," it struck an iceberg on its maiden voyage and sank two hours later, killing 1,500 people. A horrific conclusion.

When I was nine we moved to a more isolated house on Coronado Island. I found myself spending an inordinate amount of time reading and transcribing the *Encyclopedia Britannica* (God only knows why). Being a tidy child, I started with "Aardvark" and eventually made my way to "Architecture" where I found dream-like drawings of famous buildings in history. I was riveted by one of the Roman Forum, a particularly beautiful arrangement of buildings and open space crowded with people. Of course I didn't know what "Roman" or "Forum" meant. I went immediately to the R's in the encyclopedia and read about the Roman Empire, which to this day has had a tight grip on me. The article included many photographs, one being the Roman Forum in its present ruined state. I couldn't understand how in one picture the Forum was whole and beautiful, in the other a clutter of rubble.

A year or so later, living in the same house, I became aware of the actress Marilyn Monroe. She was frequently on the cover of, or featured in, the pages of *Life Magazine*. One August day I was returning from

Drawing of Marilyn Monroe by Phil Kaelin, 1969

a swim at the officer's club just down the street and encountered my brother who was on his way to the club. He stared at me, laughed, and said, "She's dead."

"Who's dead?" I asked.

"Marilyn Monroe, she killed herself," he answered.

I was shocked. When I got home I asked my mother if what my brother said was true. She said, "Yes, she committed suicide. She took her own life." I couldn't comprehend why someone so beautiful, famous and wealthy would do that. We were taught that beauty and all the rest was the key to happiness.

In a span of two years, I learned that beauty is ephemeral. A garden can be beautiful and disrespected. A great collection of buildings can be awe-inspiring one moment and vandalized and neglected the next. A beautiful person can apparently have everything that we're told matters, but fall into the depths of despair and even take their own life.

Despite these grim lessons, I knew I had the desire and drive to build and maintain beautiful things. At the same time, I realized all of it might share a destructive fate.

Sweet Peas

Winters in Coronado were cool, but never cold, and it was the perfect time to sow sweet peas. By spring the pastel-colored blossoms would fill the air with an intoxicating fragrance. My mother was in charge of growing these plants. She cut blossoms and made arrangements for the house. I was never able to grow sweet peas as well in the northeast although I try every year.

CHAPTER TWO

Mosquitoes, Stock, Lilac, Magnolia, and Ancient Rome

A Lesson in Control

In late autumn of 1962, the family moved from the Mediterranean-like splendor of San Diego County to the cold gray landscape of Alexandria, Virginia. For a year we lived in a development called Hollin Hall. Across the street was a woodland with a brook flowing through it. My brother and sisters and I spent time making low dams across the brook, which in turn created small pools. The fun was in breaking the dams and watching the water rush out of the pools. I discovered frogs which I liked to look at—but not touch. Mosquitoes and gnats were new to me. I would swat at them energetically, which only seemed to make the attacks more vigorous. I learned that if you stay calm and keep your blood flow normal they tend to show interest in some other person nearby who is flailing their arms wildly.

Gardening Badly

In autumn of 1963, we moved to a development named Collingswood and lived there until the summer of 1968. I became involved in a variety

Above: Bald cypress (*Taxodium distichum*)

of pursuits, none of them the activities of a normal teenager. The backyard of our 1960s contemporary split-level was small and closed in by a four-foot cyclone fence. Our neighbors to the rear lived in a tidy old brick house. The neighbor lady often engaged me in conversation as we stood on our respective sides of the fence. I could see she had a beautiful garden. We had no garden aside from an old gnarled chokecherry. One spring day she gave me a packet of annual stock seed. She explained how to turn over the soil and make it ready to accept the seed. I was amazed how quickly the seedlings grew. Occasionally my neighbor encouraged my efforts, "The most important thing to do to get bushy growth and more flowers is to pinch the terminal growth to cause branching." Sure enough the plants became bushier. If one pinch was good, a second pinch would be even better. I should have quit while I was ahead. With the second pinch, I managed to systematically remove all the flower buds. My first attempt at "advanced" gardening was a dismal failure.

At around the same time, my mother and I went to one of the local garden centers, just to browse. We happened upon a small lilac shrub, (*Syringa vulgaris*). My mother waxed on about the beauty and fragrance of the flowers, a memory of her childhood in Rhode Island, and then

Lilacs were among Emily Trexler's favorite plants.
In 2012 a Lilac Garden was dedicated in her memory at Tower Hill.

impulsively bought the shrub. We found a good location for it. We dug into the clayey soil and made a hole the size of the root ball, planted the shrub and then watered it in. Something told me to water the plant everyday, so I did. *Every* day. With that kind of attention the plant could do only one thing, die. And die it did. My first attempt at growing a woody plant was an outright failure.

One of the most beautiful native trees in northern Virginia is the southern magnolia (*Magnolia grandiflora*). A friend had a wooded area adjacent to his home which contained several seedlings and saplings of southern magnolia. I asked if I could have one and his mother said, "Yes." Early the following Saturday my older sister and I, with shovel in hand, went to the woodland and decided to dig a seven-foot sapling. Needless to say we had absolutely no idea what we were doing. We chopped and dug and managed to get the tree out of the ground with no soil on the roots and only about eighteen inches around the roots. We carried the tree the half-mile back to our house. We dug a hole just big enough to contain the spindly tree. True to form, I watered the tree every day. After a month the leaves began to fall off. Yet again, my efforts at gardening produced another failure.

Building Rome

During the same period, I found a book in my high school library titled *Rome and the Romans* by Grant Showerman, Professor of Classics at the University of Wisconsin, Madison, and Director of Summer Sessions at the American Academy in Rome. This book had a profound affect on me. I checked it out at least nine times, until I eventually lied and said I lost it. My mother paid the five-dollar fine and the book was mine. (In 2012 I bought another copy on Amazon for twelve dollars.) The book is profusely illustrated with photographs and drawings by two German artists, Bühlmann and Wagner. I was enamored with the drawing of the Roman Forum and I got it into my head to build a model of the Forum based on one of the drawings. I took many quarters out of my mother's wallet to purchase the building materials: poster board, typing paper,

John's model of the Roman Forum, c. 1966

Elmer's Glue and Scotch Tape. Halfway into the project I rejected the effort due to the scale and started over again. My mother would later comment how I had the "patience of Job," especially when I sculpted Corinthian capitals out of typing paper. The model took a long time to complete and occupied a large part of our family room. After several weeks, my mother mustered the courage to tell me I had to remove it for the sake of a rearrangement of furniture. I stomped the thing flat then sulked for a day. The model lives on in black and white photos, looking pretty good considering it was done by an immature fourteen-year-old.

In the same book, I was awed by a drawing of the Temple of Juno Moneta, a detail from a larger drawing by Bühlmann and Wagner. I asked a friend, Ronald Lyle, if he would copy it. I paid him twenty-five dollars from my paper route savings and supplied the material, poster board and No. 2 pencils. It took him weeks to do it but the end result was extraordinary considering he was sixteen. I had the picture framed and it remains a treasured possession.

Busted

My fascination with Rome inspired an interest in classical art. I was particularly drawn to statuary. In Hollin Hall Plaza there was a gift shop run by a pleasant fussy man who wore glasses attached with a chain around his neck—something clicked in my head that he was somehow "different." The merchandise and overwhelming fragrances of candles and potpourri intrigued me. Among the clutter of items were two twelve inch busts of composers Franz Liszt and Richard Wagner. I was enamored with classical music and especially Mozart and Beethoven. I asked the shop owner if he had busts of them and he said, "No." Drawn more to the busts themselves than to the subjects, I paid the five dollars each and carried them home in the basket of my bike. My parents were puzzled as to why their sixteen-year-old son made such a purchase but I ignored their questions, went to my bedroom and positioned the busts on my bureau. Satisfied with the effect, I now owned a little bit of faux art to appease my burgeoning obsession with all things classical.

College days, 1970

CHAPTER THREE

Taking Root

IN EARLY 1968, MY FATHER retired from the Navy and we moved to Barrington, Rhode Island, between my junior and senior year of high school. Little of importance happened until I went off to college in late August of 1969, except perhaps my many failed attempts to get into college.

I had come to the conclusion that I needed to grow up, learn a trade and get on with life. I decided I wanted to be an architect and applied to the University of Rhode Island, the Rhode Island School of Design, Drexel Institute, Pratt Institute, and the University of Massachusetts. One by one, I received polite letters of rejection. In 1969 you had two choices, college or Vietnam. My father didn't want me to go into the military and I didn't want to go to Vietnam.

My father suggested I go have a talk with my guidance counselor. Mr. Coen was aware of my five rejections and we both concluded that it was unlikely that I would become an architect. He asked what else I enjoyed doing. After some quiet thought, I answered, "Gardening."

"Ah, horticulture," he responded.

"*Horti* what?" I asked.

He explained that horticulture was, in fact, gardening and suggested I

Above: American chestnut (*Castanea dentate*)

apply to a school in Doylestown, Pennsylvania, that offered a major in it. He handed me the course catalog for Delaware Valley College of Science and Agriculture and sent me on my way. I was to return the next day and tell him my impression of the school. After I showed my parents the catalog, I went to my room to read it cover to cover. I knew, or at least thought I knew, that I wanted to major in what was called ornamental horticulture. The next day my counselor called the college admissions office and described my interest in ornamental horticulture. Delaware Valley accepted me over the phone. All I had to do was go through the formality of the application process. A week later I graduated from Barrington High.

Summer went by quickly. I was occupied by my job as a hospital janitor and on days off sailed with my sister on Narragansset Bay. I dreamed of escaping to college.

When college began the last week of August 1969, I was determined to make new friends and be part of a like-minded family.

Ginkgo Stinko

The first few weeks were taken up by the hazing period. Freshmen wore silly beanies called "dinks" and had to do whatever any sophomore told us to do. In the center of the Delaware Valley campus, there was an allée of Ginkgo trees (*Gingko biloba*). Gingkos are dioecious meaning some trees are male and others female. The females are known for bearing foul-smelling fruit and the trees in the allée were all female. Two sophomores instructed me to hop on one foot the length of the allée. I politely said, "No." They said I had to. I refused, less politely this time.

"Do it!" they demanded.

My response, which was something like "Go fuck yourselves," was not well-received.

The following Saturday before a football game, my punishment was to kneel on one knee and sing the school song. I have a pretty good voice, so my rendition was applauded. The glee club later solicited me.

As classes began in earnest, reality slowly sank in. You went to college to learn a skill that would lead to a career, one that would give you the ability to live independently and pay taxes. In my freshman year I was exposed to careers in ornamental horticulture that were then available: golf course superintendent, landscape contractor, nursery manager, arborist, florist. I realized after that first year that none of those careers appealed to me.

The school required that you work nine months at a job relating to your major and I decided to take a position as a grounds keeper on campus. It appealed to me more than going home and gave me the opportunity to spend time in Philadelphia, thirty minutes away by train. The job mostly entailed mowing and weeding, but one day I was ordered to dig a semi-circular bed flanking a path leading to the administration building and plant it with red geraniums. The bed turned out a bit misshapen but so was the path that gave it its outline. When I finished, I stood back to examine it. I thought it looked odd. Just then the assistant dean drove by, stopped, rolled down the window, stared long and hard at the bed of geraniums, then at me, and stuttered, "That looks like hell." He rolled up the window and drove off. My first effort at landscape design was pronounced a definitive failure.

The Beacon Hill House

On my one trip home that summer, I attempted to visit an estate called the Beacon Hill House in Newport. I had discovered it in a book on historic landscape architecture at the college library. The photographs revealed a garden of great beauty located in the rocky terrain of the Newport coastline, although it was set back from the famous Ocean Drive. The garden was designed by the Olmstead Brothers and owned by Arthur Curtis James. One morning I borrowed my parents' car, drove the forty-five minutes to Newport and found the area where I thought the garden might be located, to no avail. I knocked on doors and asked whomever responded if they knew where the home of Arthur Curtis James was—the Beacon Hill house to be specific. No one had any idea of what I was referring to. Eventually, I stopped in front of a house that was almost hidden from the street, parked, and with some apprehension walked up the gravel driveway. It was clear that someone had entered the driveway too fast and made ruts, spraying gravel into the shrub plantings on either side. One of the granite bollards flanking the entrance had been knocked over and broken. I rang the doorbell and waited. The man who answered was about my age with a scratch on his face and a prominent black eye. Nervously I asked if he knew of the Beacon Hill House. He said, "No," but told me to wait a moment. A few minutes later an older man appeared, "I understand you're looking for the Beacon Hill House."

"Yes," I said.

"It was burned down years ago. What's left is across the street."

Sure enough, diagonally across the street were two impressive gateposts with a chain between them. I resituated my car on the street and began my adventure. I quickly deduced that this was a service entrance because I found the remains of greenhouses and cold frames. Like the Roman Forum, the Beacon Hill House was in ruins. Beyond the dilapidated greenhouses I found natural stone steps leading up to a high point and the remains of a limestone belvedere with a view of the ocean. It was complete with a mosaic compass rose. A bit further I located a second natural stone stairway that led down to the remains of a cypress lattice screen and gate posts into what was the Blue Garden—so beautifully illustrated in the book from the library. I kicked away years of accumulated leaves to find blue tile and limestone-edged pools.

The outline of the garden was still visible. Cryptomeria trees, which once served as evergreen screens, still remained. Another path led past where the house must have stood. Beyond were the remnants of Mrs. James' rose garden, where climbing roses with yellow flowers had miraculously survived. There was a circular pool, an overlook, and a curved staircase leading down to further sections of the rose garden. A pool directly below the overlook had once been filled by water cascading over the millstone above. I continued until I found myself out in the open, standing on what must have been a great lawn leading up to

The Beacon Hill House, from a postcard published in 1920
Courtesy Library of Congress

the house. From there I exited through the former main entrance and followed the road until my car appeared in the distance.

I was both exhilarated and saddened by what I had seen. I fantasized about owning such a property and restoring it to its former glory.

Finding a Direction

In my sophomore year, I became friends with a senior, Tom Buchter, who clearly knew what direction his education would take him. In contrast, I couldn't even figure out how to spend my summer. Tom suggested I apply for a job at Ringwood, a state park in northern New Jersey that had beautiful landscape gardens. I applied and was hired.

Tom Buchter and John, 1978

Ringwood State Park comprises approximately 16,000 acres. Primarily woodland, it contributes in part to the Wanaque Reservoir watershed. There are three large recreation areas: Erskine Lake, Ringwood Manor, and Skylands Manor. Ringwood Manor was the former country estate of the Cooper-Hewitt family and Skylands was the former summer home of Clarence McKenzie Lewis. Skylands was more interesting horticulturally, although Ringwood had a storied history going back to the late eighteenth century. I spent most of that first summer at Ringwood, weeding the beds around the house and cutting out invasive vines at the top of the large terrace garden, which was adjacent to, but had no relationship with, the manor house. My most memorable experiences at Ringwood involved poison ivy and pruning lilac.

The poison ivy was growing above the wall at the far end of the lower terrace. God only knows why I got it in my head to pull this vine out with my bare hands, but I did. There was hardly a square inch of my body that wasn't affected. With the help of calamine lotion and perseverance, it slowly went away. I later learned from Euell Gibbons' book, *Stalking the Wild Asparagus*, that if you eat three leaves of poison ivy

The lilac at the entrance to Ringwood State Park, 2016

every day for three weeks in early spring, you will develop immunity. I followed the formula and I'm happy to say it worked—although everyone thought I was out of my mind. I have not had a case of poison ivy since.

The lilac (*Syringa vulgaris*), located near the front gate, consisted of an exceptionally large colony of old gnarled trunks at least fifteen feet in height. One Saturday I decided to "rejuvenate" it. I began thinning out the oldest and, by the way, the most beautiful trunks. I sawed and sawed until I was completely exhausted. The end result was a thin thicket of small amorphic young growth. I had butchered the once noble planting—another horticultural failure.

Working at Ringwood gave me the opportunity to take a walk through the terrace gardens at Skylands with the superintendent of the park. Somewhat arrogantly, he rattled off the names of each shrub. To my surprise I remembered the name of every plant. Plant binomials became a new and second language.

That summer I came to the realization that public horticulture was my career path. I was stimulated by the restoration of fine old gardens. The work gave me the opportunity to take care of a great variety of plants as well as meet and talk to visitors. I enjoyed answering their questions and giving them gardening tips.

Thanks to Tom's suggestion that I work at Ringwood, I developed a true sense of purpose and professional goals as I started my junior year. I returned to Ringwood the next summer and worked directly with Tom at Skylands Manor. That summer opened my eyes to the genius of the place.

Francis Lynde Stetson (1846-1920), legal consultant to J.P. Morgan, had pieced together Skylands from a collection of eighteenth century farms. His intention was to create a summer getaway from his Manhattan home. His landscape architect, Samuel Parsons, designed a comprehensive farm with an enormous barn and houses for staff dotted the 1,100 acres. Stetson's impressive residence was built on a large level area at the foot of a hill called Mt. Defiance. A golf enthusiast, Stetson commissioned the design of a nine hole course adjacent to the mansion, interspersed with formal gardens and shrub plantings. A beautiful man-made pond acted as a water trap for the course. Parsons received an award from the American Society of Landscape Architects, an organization he helped to found, for the naturalistic design of the pond.

The overall effect of the estate was of great natural beauty. The property was accessible by miles of groomed dirt roads, and barns of varying sizes and pastures and fields accommodated cattle, horses, sheep, goats, ducks and chickens. There was even an abattoir for butchering. A carriage house and garage, and a pump house to provide water for the house, gardens, and golf course completed the complex.

Francis Stetson died in 1920. With no heirs the estate went on the market. Clarence MacKenzie Lewis (1877-1959), an acquaintance of Stetson's who lived just over the mountain in Mahwah, New Jersey, and his mother Helen Lewis Salomon, widow of banker William A. Salomon, had had their eye on Skylands for some time. When it came on the market, they were quick to buy it. They had initially wanted

Taking Root

The front façade of Skylands as it looked in 1936

to build a residence in the exclusive development of Tuxedo Park but were discouraged from doing so because Salomon was Jewish. Their goal was to raze the Stetson house and build a Tudor showplace designed by John Russell Pope along with a garden of enormous scale. Although Helen Salomon died in 1924 before the house was complete, Lewis went on to finish the house and landscape. Landscape architect Alfred Geiffert (1890-1957), designed a harmonious collection of formal gardens, sweeping lawns, and groves of trees. Lewis himself with his gardening staff laid out the more naturalistic gardens. The end result was considered to be the finest private garden in America. The garden themes were of three types: ornamental, economic, and ecologic. The two latter were separated from the former by a half-mile allée of 220 standard hybrid crabapple trees (*Malus x atrosanguinea*).

Coincidentally, John Russell Pope and Alfred Geiffert had also collaborated on the National Gallery of Art in Washington, D.C., a building I admired as a teenager living in Alexandria. I rode my motor scooter

John at Skylands, 1974

many a time to visit the gallery and take in its classical splendor.

Clarence Lewis owned Skylands from 1920 to 1953. At the age of seventy-six he sold the property to Shelton College, a private religious institution, for a mere $250,000. The college was poor and had no ability to maintain the buildings, gardens, or the extensive infrastructure. Skylands quickly slipped into neglect and disrepair. Because of its proximity to Ringwood State Park, Skylands was acquired by the State of New Jersey in 1966. Clarence Lewis' head gardener, Stuart Longmuir, had been retained by the college and knew every nook and cranny of the place. The state poured millions of dollars into restoration. Stuart eventually taught me two very important lessons: 1. When backing-up a vehicle, only go as far as you need to make a desired turn. 2. When making a curve on a bed or border, be sure it doesn't exceed a train's ability to make such a curve.

In 1971, I became part of a team working on the restoration of Skylands. Until I left in 1978, I had the pleasure of restoring the Lilac Garden, Inner Park, Bog Garden, Cactus Garden, and Wildflower Garden. I oversaw the propagation greenhouse which grew 14,000 annual flowers every year. We also propagated hundreds of species of shrubs and trees by cutting and seed which were disseminated to other public gardens or to interested gardeners. My time at Skylands would have a profound influence on me for the remainder of my career.

Gloria Gunnera

In February of 1976, I took a six-week vacation without pay to Munich, Germany, with overnights to Bonn, Frankfurt, Cologne, and Tubingen. I asked Tom Buchter if he wanted me to bring back anything special.

"Yes," he responded, "a Gunnera seedling."

Gunnera is a South American herbaceous perennial that can grow to eight feet with leaves six feet across. Back then the plant was a kind of "holy grail" of horticulture. On one of my last days in Munich I visited the Munich Botanical Garden (Botanischer Garten) and had a private tour with a Herr Dr. Mueller who was generous with both his time

The Gunnera flourishing at Skylands, 1977

and information. During our walk, I noticed two large dormant plantings of Gunnera (*Gunnera tinctoria*) partly covered by large wooden boxes. I asked Herr Mueller if I could possibly obtain a small division of Gunnera. Without hesitation he said, "Yes." I picked up the division the day before I left for home. At least a cubic foot in size, it was far larger than I expected. My friend Stuart Simon who I had been staying with helped me clean all the soil off the roots and carefully box the plant. We tied the box with twine for easy carrying.

Without a plant import permit, it was a gamble whether or not I would get through customs in Boston. With some fancy foot work and good old fashioned begging, the plant was permitted to go through. At my parents' home in Barrington, Rhode Island, I planted the division in a large pot using my father's outstanding compost, drove back to Skylands and placed it in the warm greenhouse where we started annuals. Tom was delighted. In late April we planted the Gunnera along

The West Lawn at Skylands, 1975

the stream in the Bog Garden on a hummock formed from Skylands compost. It grew beautifully that first year. The second year it was five feet high.

When I left Skylands for the Park Commission in 1978, I took a division of the Gunnera with me and it thrived. Later, during a tour that I led for a local garden club, I noticed in the distance a friend, Bill Whitaker, and his wife admiring the giant plant. Catching sight of me, Bill shouted in a loud distinct voice, "Hey John, where did you get the *gonorrhea?*" The garden club gave a collective gasp. Without hesitation, I shouted back, "Munich, Germany!"

I brought a division of that same plant with me when I moved to Massachusetts. Now all three plants have gone to that heavenly compost pile in the sky.

Sore Loser

Though I was happy at Skylands, I felt I needed a job with more responsibility and benefits. I applied for the position of garden director at the Garden in the Woods in Framingham, Massachusetts. When the deadline for the interviewing process had passed, I was the top contender, so I was surprised to hear that the job was awarded to someone else. However disappointed, I reasoned that I had a stable and secure job at Skylands. A few weeks later, I took a trip to Duke University in Durham, North Carolina, to visit my college roommate Norman Finnance and his wife. While on a walk in the Sarah Duke Garden on campus, we came across a rather taciturn gardener working in one of the native plant borders. I kept peppering him with questions to get him to talk. Eventually, he asked me where I worked. I replied that I was restoring the wildflower garden at Skylands. He stared at me and said, "You must be John Trexler."

It dawned on me that this man was David Longland who had been appointed director at the Garden in the Woods. Without preamble, I exclaimed, "You sonofabitch!" raised my right foot and pushed him into the border. This sounds terrible but it was done with good humor. Dave and I became friends and have stayed connected. Go figure.

High Anxiety

Skylands was a near perfect garden. No detail was too small to consider when planting the immense landscape. The landscape surrounding the house was simple, but every plant was located to the precise inch so that it could mature properly and compliment the large structure. A given plant had a thoughtful relationship to its coinciding plant. When you travelled around the house from front to back, north to south, you were greeted by a mature red maple (*Acer rubrum*). The tree was perfectly proportioned to the house. Its distance from the house was approximately one third the width of the lawn on which it was located. The tree complimenting it to the west was on the other side of a low retaining wall. When you walked around to the south lawn, the two trees framed the view. This level of continuous harmony with plants that change and grow is credit to the skill of the gardeners that sited and planted them. In the mid-seventies the red maple began to die from the top down, always a bad sign. The tree had a "girdling" root that was choking it. A decision was made to cut the maple down and a brief meeting was held to determine what the replacement tree should be. I suggested another red maple.

"An English oak," sang the majority.

"No, it will grow too big," I warned. "Okay, an English oak but it has to be planted in the exact same spot as the maple to preserve the harmony established fifty years earlier."

"No, it's too much work to remove the stump," the majority ruled.

"But we have to respect the historic landscape—the artistry!" I pleaded.

Deaf ears were turned; the English oak was planted. The oak is now huge and hogs the once beautifully framed view. When I visit this spot, I avert my eyes and visualize the landscape as it once was—perfect.

The restored Pool Garden at Bamboo Brook, 1980

Because of my particular status with the State of New Jersey, my job came with no official title, no health insurance, no sick time, no personal time and no vacation. I was twenty-six and needed to find employment that would give me more security. The Morris County Park Commission offered me the position of superintendent of horticulture. In June of 1978, I moved the fifty miles south to Morristown, and began my second job. The Park Commission hired me to oversee horticultural activity at eighteen parks. However, they were primarily interested in the restoration of the private garden of the late Martha Brookes (Brown) Hutcheson (1871–1959), Merchiston Farm, a.k.a. Bamboo Brook.

Five of the hundred acres that made up Bamboo Brook were devoted to formal gardens. The layout, though much more rustic, was not dissimilar to Skylands. There is little doubt that Mrs. Hutcheson was familiar with Clarence Lewis and his nationally acclaimed estate and had visited on the days it was open to the public. Martha Hutcheson began laying out her garden in 1916, Lewis in 1924. The common thread were the many axes: parallel, perpendicular, and diagonal. They both understood the continuity and opportunity axial layout provides. In many ways Skylands was an easier landscape to restore. The Bamboo Brook garden was "muddy," the details not as clearly defined. The time I spent solving the problems of and restoring Bamboo Brook itself was a joy. The odd tug of war in which my supervisor was engaged with his supervisor was not. After six years of internal "politics," I was ready to move on.

Master Planning

The last year I was employed by the Park Commission, I participated in a master planning process for Bamboo Brook and an adjacent property Willowood Arboretum. There had always been a neighborly connection between the two properties. Martha Hutcheson was friendly with the Tubb Brothers who owned Willowood. Russ Meyers, Secretary Director of the Park Commission, rightly felt it would be a win-win if the properties became a dual experience for the casual visitor and share educational programming, plant accessions and overall interpretation. After several interviews the Philadelphia-based Andropogon Associates were chosen to do the plan. I participated in group meetings and one-on-ones with the principle landscape architects. The end result was a shared path that crossed Bamboo Brook that could accommodate maintenance vehicles as well as foot traffic. The path logically approached both landscapes at key entry points. A common thread was the similarities of architecture and garden style. Months of time and tens of thousands of dollars were spent to create the plan. Unfortunately, it ended up in a desk drawer never to see the light of day again. I was appalled by the outcome of this thorough and thoughtful process. I promised myself that if I ever participated in a master planning process again, I would be sure to see it come to fruition.

*Before WCHS formally bought the property in March 1986,
Tony King took photographs of the Tower Hill snowscape.*
Photo by Tony King, 1986

CHAPTER FOUR

Right Place, Right Time

An Eventful Evening

At the annual (1983) Christmas party of the Hortus Club of New York held in Manhattan, I sat between two friends, Charlie Mazza and Elizabeth Scholtz, Education Director and President respectively of the Brooklyn Botanic Garden. They conversed across me about Fred Roberts, who was leaving his job as director of the Worcester County Horticultural Society (WCHS) in Worcester, Massachusetts, and taking on the director's job at Longwood Gardens, Kennett Square, Pennsylvania. The executive director's job in Worcester was advertised in the latest newsletter of the American Association of Botanical Gardens and Arboreta (the AABGA, now the APGA, the American Public Garden Association).

When I returned home, I looked up the listing in the newsletter. After a pow-wow with my partner, Bob Zeleniak, I wrote a cover letter and submitted my resume. The following week I called the Horticultural Society office to see if they had received my letter, and since I was going to be in the area the following week anyway, proposed that I stop by and

Above: American elm (*Ulmus americana*))

Fred Roberts
From the WCHS Newsletter, 1983

introduce myself. My friend Tom Buchter from Skylands had recently moved to Massachusetts to take on the job of executive director at the New England Wild Flower Society (NEWFS). I asked him if I could come up and spend a night and then I would go the following day and introduce myself to Fred. He and his wife Kent were happy to put me up.

Fred had warned that Worcester was a maze of one-way streets, so I paid close attention as I approached the headquarters of WCHS at 30 Elm Street. After a couple of tries, I found my way to the parking lot behind the building on time. As I entered at the Chestnut Street door I couldn't believe my eyes. The building was elegant and beautifully appointed. Fred was cordial and folksy. He led me through the paneled library up three steps to his office which was a veritable parade chamber. We sat opposite each other in chairs on either side of a fireplace. Once we were settled, he was quick to point out that I had misspelled "horticulturist" in my letter of introduction. I had spelled it "horticulturalist" with an extra syllable. That detail put aside, we began my informal interview. He outlined a brief history of WCHS and discussed their plans to develop a comprehensive horticultural center. I gave an in-depth history of my career in public horticulture and emphasized the skills I felt complimented the goals of the Society. The interview lasted an hour and a half. Afterward I returned to New Jersey.

Fred called a few days later to let me know I was one of three finalists. He requested that I come back for a formal meeting with the search committee and have lunch with the president of the Society. I was encouraged and excited.

Once again I sat in Fred's office, this time faced by the five-member search committee. They barraged me with questions. I felt comfortable and relaxed and questioned them in return to get a sense of their commitment to the development of a public garden. It was a major decision for Bob and me to move to Massachusetts and begin a new life away from New Jersey. I needed to know their level of seriousness.

After the interview, I went to the Worcester Club with Cushing "Cush" Bozenhard, President of the Board of Trustees. The club had been the private home of an early president of WCHS and was elegant and more than a little intimidating. Cush put me at ease straightaway and questioned me about my vision for the proposed center. My response was that it was a complex question that required information about the needs of the community and the general goals of the region. Lunch ended and I headed back to New Jersey.

I kept my fingers crossed. Fred called a few days later to say that the full board wanted to meet me. I was to give a thirty-minute talk on some general ideas for a horticultural center. Back I went with a carousel of slides and well-rehearsed text. I enjoyed giving the presentation and presumed that my audience was riveted. When the lights went on, thirty lifeless faces stared up at me. I attempted to snap life back into them by asking if there were questions. Nothing. Then a petite lady sitting in the front row, wearing a full-length mink coat and dark glasses, raised her hand, "What was the plant with the silver flowers in the thirty-seventh slide?" she asked.

Helen Stoddard (right), friend and benefactor of the Worcester County Horticultural Society, in her renowned garden in Worcester with British horticulturist Rosemary Verey, 1994

Without hesitation, I said, "*Stenanthium gramminium* variety *robustum*." "Spell it!" she demanded and I did.

The Q&A ended and the room emptied except for the lady in the mink coat. She asked me to repeat the spelling of the plant. She thanked me, said my talk was "marvelous," and left the room. Cush led me downstairs to Fred's office and told me I had done a good job and had also done the right thing by answering the lady's question (what else was I supposed to do?). He then said, "She's Helen Stoddard and she's going to bankroll the project." I thought he was putting the cart before the horse. Nobody is going to invest in the Society's ambitious plans until they know precisely what those plans are. I got in my car and drove back to New Jersey.

Right Place, Right Time

Apparently

For all intents and purposes, the trustees of WCHS wanted to hire a Renaissance man with a multitude of skills. In me, they got an educator and horticulturist. I had an intense interest in history, had restored and designed gardens, and knew that form follows function when designing buildings. I was able to communicate with prospective donors and understood process—not losing site of the ultimate goal. And, last but not least, I was not a micro-manager. A pretty good skill set for their needs.

A week later, Cush informed me that I had received twenty-nine out of thirty votes from the trustees in favor of my becoming executive director. He offered me $30,000 and I asked for $35,000. He hesitated and then said if all went well they would raise my salary to $35,000 after six months. We agreed on a starting date of Monday, April 16, 1984. Back to Worcester I went one more time, before officially beginning the job, to attend the preview party of the annual spring flower show and to find a place for my partner, Bob Zeleniak, and I to live.

Bob's only criterion was that the apartment be "cool." I looked at several and settled on an adequate—not so cool—two bedroom, first floor corner unit at 30 Cedar Street, a five-minute walk from WCHS headquarters on Elm Street. Bob followed the moving van up to Worcester on Monday, April 9. I drove up on Friday the 13th. When I arrived, Bob greeted me with an article from the *Worcester Telegram and Gazette* with the headline "Bozenhard Resigns from Horticultural Society Board." The article also said that the secretary and the education coordinator had resigned. Yikes, what the hell was going on?

During the time I applied and was accepted to be the director of WCHS, Skylands was designated the New Jersey State Botanical Garden. For several years friends of Skylands and I had lobbied with Governor Tom Kean and officials at the Parks and Forestry Department of the state. I am quoted as saying, "This will ensure the future of one of the finest horticultural collections in the country." I left New Jersey on a high point.

On Monday the 16th, I dressed in a suit and tie and made my way

Bob Zeleniak, always "cool," 1981

to the main entrance of the Horticulture Building in Worcester. The door was locked. I knocked and rang the doorbell, no response. I went around to the back entrance and that door was locked as well. I knocked, no response. I went back to the main entrance, still locked.

I stood there perplexed. What had I gotten myself into? I then heard a voice say, "Hello, Mr. Trexler." It was Gary Cippro, the education coordinator who had resigned the previous Friday along with the administrative secretary. He had realized that the trustees had asked me to start at 8:30 a.m. on the 16th. It was Patriots Day in Massachusetts and a state holiday. The Society was closed. He apologized on behalf of the organization, gave me his keys and security code and left me to fend for myself.

Right Place, Right Time

The Horticulture Building at 30 Elm Street in Worcester

There I was—alone—in this palatial building. I called Bob and said I would be home for lunch. In the interim I settled at my desk and put out my nameplate and pen set from the Park Commission. Then I got up and explored the building. I started on the second floor, checking every room and closet and repeated the exercise on the first floor, basement and sub-basement where the furnace was located. As I made my way through the 25,000 square feet of the building, I passed a series of portraits with gilded frames of distinguished men. I assumed they must have had important connections to the Society.

I studied the library, discovered many floor level cabinets and began an investigation. The cabinets contained books—old books, *very* old books—the oldest dated back to December 14, 1499. They had thick layers of dust which led me to believe they had not been handled for decades. I methodically wiped each book clean and made a list of titles.

TRANSACTIONS

During this library discovery time, I found the *Transactions of the Worcester County Horticultural Society*, annual histories written from 1840 to 1977, but dropped from 1978 to 1983. I decided then and there to resurrect the tradition and directed my staff to compile transactions throughout my tenure at WCHS, 1984 to 2011.

On that first day, the phone rang once. It was the vice president of the board, Isabel Arms, a member of the search committee (who later dubbed me "benign dictator"). She also had realized they had asked me to start on a day the Society was closed. She was apologetic and wished me well. It was clear there was no plan or agenda to handle my arrival but I kept myself occupied. It became apparent to me that I had to understand the history of the Society in order to thoughtfully accomplish the stated goals. My time was well spent on that unceremonious first day and I made a point of getting a better picture of why and how the trustees had reached the decision to build a public garden. The following is what I learned.

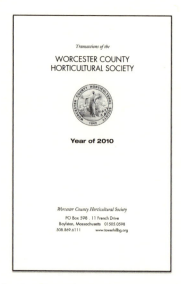

With the Transaction Reports, John continued a tradition established by the early founders to record the yearly events and financial records of the Society.

Right Place, Right Time

Public Garden Genesis

The executive committee met October 12, 1982 at the Horticultural Building on Elm Street. The following are the minutes from that meeting as recorded by Board Secretary Ernestine W. Blanchard. Executive Director Kenn Stephens and former President of the Board Paul Rogers shared their outline for the future of WCHS. In their view, the Society suffered from:

> Inadequate finances with no long-range security,
> Image,
> Low participation from both members and general public,
> Inadequate staff,
> Physical plant (building too large for most occasions and too small for the Spring Flower Show).

They suggested three plans for consideration:

> Maintain present programs that are popular with the members (shows, lecture series, holiday decoration classes, annual meeting, etc.) and add outreach programs geared to youth, elderly, etc.
>
> Develop a horticulture center in an accessible location in conjunction with commercial participation. The present building would not be needed for this program.
>
> Join another organization such as the Hadwen Arboretum at Clark University.

The minutes went on to say:

> Current problems and future possibilities will be shared with the trustees at the October 28th meeting. President Hurlburt will call a special Trustees Meeting for Thursday, December 9, 1982 (10:00 AM) to hear Trustee comments and/or suggestions on the future direction of the Society.

A few days before that meeting on October 6, 1982, Kenn and Waite interviewed Jonathan Shaw, who at the time was executive director of the New England Wild Flower Society, to see if he would be interested in formally interviewing for the executive director's job at WCHS, as Kenn's successor, Jonathan declined the offer. He was not convinced that WCHS's future was promising.

I couldn't find minutes for an October 28th meeting. There were minutes for a meeting on November 6th, where it was reported that Kenn Stephens tendered his resignation. It was agreed it would be in the best interest of the Society to accept it. His last day was to be November 30, 1982. Kenn was honored at a luncheon on December 4th at Waite's home. He was presented with a gold Cross pen and pencil set.

The Executive Committee met on November 15, 1982 with a select group of supporters, including representatives of the Bigelow (Bigelow Nursery) and Mezitt (Weston Nursery) families. They supported modifications to the Society's operation. There were no details contained in the minutes. The consensus was, however, to keep WCHS alive.

At a meeting of the Executive Committee on December 14, 1982, it was reported that Paul Rogers would contact Fred Roberts, Director of the Kingwood Horticultural Center in Mansfield, Ohio, about a slide presentation on the development of a horticulture center. Paul knew Fred through the Garden Writers Association, and was impressed by what he had accomplished at Kingwood. Fred gave his presentation on January 27 and 28, 1983 to the full board and invited guests. He stated, "a study of properties and possible financial sources is paramount, combined with a long-range goal, meticulously planned and specifically outlined." Board members accepted Fred's suggestion that if the direction of the Society is toward a horticulture center, the new director should be on hand early enough to be involved in the selection of land and basic planning. Fred indicated that he would be interested in the position and could be available on short notice. All members were in agreement that if the Society moved in the direction of a horticulture center, WCHS would be the governing body.

On February 2, 1983, trustees Paul Rogers and Alden Miller offered their ideas on what a horticulture center should encompass. Fred presented his written outline on February 21, 1983. Paul's report is featured in the appendix of this book. Alden's report was one paragraph and was enclosed in Paul's report.

—⚍—

The trustees voted to authorize the executive committee to conclude arrangements with Fred as Executive Director of WCHS. Fred started working part-time in late May 1983, and started full-time in late July. At the October 26, 1983 Executive Committee meeting, Fred announced he had been selected to succeed Everett L. Miller as director of Longwood Gardens, Kennett Square, Pennsylvania, the preeminent public garden in the United States. He agreed to assume that post in mid-1984. In the interim he would concentrate on the development of the New England Horticulture Center and help find a successor. The following is a summary of Fred's outline titled, "An Outline For The Development of a Horticulture Center, Sponsored by the Worcester County Horticultural Society, February 21, 1983."

Objectives:
1. Promote public interest in and knowledge of horticulture as both an art and a science.
2. Provide opportunities for individual participation in horticulture that are educational, enjoyable, and culturally enriching.
3. Promote and distribute plant materials of merit to increase their availability to the gardening public.
4. Contribute to research in horticulture through field-testing new plant varieties, agricultural chemicals, cultural techniques, and new tools and equipment.

The site selected should be adjacent to core populations, convenient to a highway, 50+ acres, have a buffering woodland, have adequate water for human use and irrigation, adequate potential for septic, good soil, radical changes in topography and significant natural vegetation. The development of a master plan for the center is essential. The center should be designed with consideration given to New England architectural style in both buildings and gardens. Respect and protect the existing library. Site preparation would include the layout and development of an access road. Establishment of an endowment fund is essential.

Fred exited on May 4, 1984. The outline was his legacy and the guide I used as WCHS took the next step with me as its executive director.

—⚭—

I was quick to hire an administrative assistant, Diane Paradis, who came equipped with all the skills we required, including knowledge of computers. Up to that point the Society owned two IBM electric typewriters. With the guidance of Henry Rudio, the Society's treasurer, we acquired a Compaq computer, a machine compatible with Henry's company, KMG Main Hurdman's, system. The computer was used for bookkeeping and word processing.

At a special tea on June 27th, I was introduced to the presidents of the local garden clubs. It was clear that having a close connection with garden clubs was essential to further the goal of developing a public garden. I also learned that there were two distinct organizations of garden clubs, the Garden Club Federation of Massachusetts and the Garden Club of America. There were some differences but their common objectives of improving gardening skills made the Society's association with them paramount.

Some disgruntled members were adamant about WCHS remaining in Worcester. Ida Brucie, an elderly lady who lived in the neighborhood of the horticultural society's headquarters, was the most vocal. I invited her to my office so I could better understand her reason for wanting the institution to stay in Worcester. She revealed that she did not have a car and depended on public transportation. I assured her we would try very hard to choose a spot that was accessible to the WRTA.

Bernice Heald

While attending the Spring Show preview at 30 Elm Street, I was introduced to various people by Cush Bozenhard. As we approached a diminutive lady—who seemed to possess a permanent scowl—Cush whispered, "I want you to meet an important person. She's the matriarch of one of Worcester's old families."

Cush presented me. "Mrs. Heald, I would like you to meet John Trexler our newly hired Executive Director."

Mrs. Heald held out her hand, "I'm prepared not to like you."

Without pause I shook her hand, looked her in the eye and said, "Well, Mrs. Heald, I'm prepared to like *you.*"

Bernice was part of the "never leave the city" group. I represented a change of which she was uncertain. Bernice and I became fast friends. On one visit she shared what she thought was a fact, that people didn't like her. She made me promise to attend her funeral and sit in the front row. She was no nonsense. I liked that about her.

That third week in April when I stepped in, there was no board president, no education coordinator and no administrative secretary. There was a full time custodian and a librarian who worked two days a month. My first order of business was to hire a secretary and work with the Executive Committee to choose a new board president from the body of four vice presidents. They were all resistant. Phil Beals was the least resistant—he felt badly that my introduction to WCHS was so awkward. He was elected president at the May 17th board meeting. Cush Bozenhard's resignation was accepted at the same meeting. As it turned out, Phil and I developed a natural rapport.

My first major task was to evaluate the fifteen properties Fred had identified as possible locations for the horticulture center. On June 4, 1984, Phil and I organized a site search committee. It consisted of nine trustees, divided into groups of three. Each group set out to evaluate five of the fifteen properties. I had composed an evaluation sheet based on the criteria in Fred's outline and the goal was to visit each property and determine how many of the criteria were met. Getting the committee members organized to do the evaluation was a bit like herding cats. When the committee reported to the board on August 27th, not one of the properties was considered a viable choice. I was instructed to identify additional properties.

Politics

I don't consider myself a political person, but I do enjoy politics. In 1984 I supported the democratic nominees, Walter Mondale and Geraldine Ferraro. At an investment meeting in the executive committee meeting room at 30 Elm Street, the presidential race became part of the discussion. I expressed my support for the Democratic team. You would have thought I'd set the room on fire. The other members of the committee jumped down my throat and made it quite clear what their politics were. I learned never to say anything the least bit political in my new surroundings.

—⚜—

In August, I made one of my best hires, Karen Perkins, a graduate of the Longwood program at the University of Delaware. Karen was smart and came with a remarkable set of skills. Her job was to coordinate the education program, manage the flower shows, and edit the newsletter. Karen and I shared many memorable times.

Karen Perkins at the annual plant sale she helped to establish at Tower Hill

Right Place, Right Time

Martinis and Hot Buttered Rolls

The Hort building was rented for parties and had a sizable kitchen where caterers often left behind goodies, including gin and vermouth, Parker House rolls and pads of butter. No one kept an inventory, so Karen and I got in the habit of helping ourselves. Our Friday late afternoon treats were a small bonus after a long work week.

Mend-a-Book

Juggling as many balls as possible, I organized a fundraising event for the care of the Society's rare books, the ones I had discovered on my first day. We called it Mend-a-Book. Invitations were designed to look like books with band-aids attached. We invited Barry Ferguson from New York, to be our guest lecturer. Barry was a renowned flower arranger and traveler. In the afternoon he performed a floral design demonstration, in the evening a travelog on a recent trip to China. We netted $10,000 for the establishment of a restricted fund for the care and restoration of worn books.

Dog and Pony Show

In order to illustrate the development of a horticulture center to prospective property owners, we created a dog and pony show in the form of slides. One property we entertained was Chedco Farm in Berlin, the country estate of Charles Edward Cotting, an old friend of Phil Beals. Phil and I drove to Mr. Cotting's office in Boston's financial district, with screen and slide projector in hand. We were greeted by his assistant who helped set up my equipment. In his nineties, Mr. Cotting seemed attentive or at least I couldn't detect whether or not he dozed off. Our goal, of course, was to see if he would have an interest in donating a portion of his property to the Horticultural Society. The answer came later in the form of a letter, a definitive, "No."

During the holiday flower show in December 1984, I received a phone call from an anonymous caller regarding a property he thought would be perfect for our goals. I asked where the property was located. He couldn't tell me. How could I possibly evaluate the land if he wouldn't tell me the location? He capitulated and told me it was in Boylston, Massachusetts, but if I wanted more specifics, I was to ask at the general store in Boylston Center. Scratching my head, I politely said, "Thank you," and hung up. When I mentioned this call to Linda Milton, a member of the board, she was sure the anonymous caller was referencing a farm called Tower Hill. Another organization she was involved with, The Trustees of Reservations (TTOR), was evaluating Tower Hill for acquisition. On December 31, 1994, Linda, my partner Bob and I met at Legal Sea Foods in Worcester, and after a few beers and bowls of chowder, drove out to Boylston to look at Tower Hill. It was love at first sight. However, the property was under serious consideration by TTOR. The owner, Mrs. Maynard Carter, had passed away in late 1983 and her executors were in charge of the sale of the land.

Helen Stoddard had become a good friend and was exceedingly interested in our finding the right location. Her husband Robert, who was closely associated with the Worcester Science Center (now the Ecotarium), was convinced that land owned by the Science Center across the street from their main campus might be a good site for the Horticulture Center. With good reason, he thought that locating a public garden adjacent to a general science museum was a practical idea and would appeal to the local donor base. We arranged to meet at the Science Center and look at the vacant land. After the tour we both felt the predominant geology was not conducive to the culture of a garden. As a sad postscript, Robert Stoddard died from heart failure a few hours after our meeting.

Around the same time, I received a call from Richard Mirick, a lawyer and trustee of Clark University in Worcester. Dick told me about the twenty-seven acre Hadwen Arboretum, owned by Clark. The arboretum had been the home and garden of Obadiah Hadwen, a past president of the Horticultural Society. In his 1907 will, Mr. Hadwen bequeathed his

A view of the Tower Hill barn and Farmhouse, c. 1986

estate at the corner of June and Lovell streets to Clark University, his farm to the city of Worcester for use as a park, and to the Horticultural Society, he gave one thousand dollars and a Victorian tall clock.

Mr. Hadwen's desire was for Clark University to maintain his collection of trees for the study of arboriculture. The university used the estate building for faculty housing and, in conjunction with the Hadwen Botanical Club, maintained the arboretum for study. Ultimately, the house was razed and pushed into the cellar hole and the arboretum became overwhelmed with weeds and Norway maple trees.

The impression given by Mr. Mirick was that the university would deed the arboretum to the Horticultural Society and thereby honor Hadwen's wish for the property to be used for educational purposes. This idea had its appeal. The Society could keep its building on Elm Street, and develop a horticulture center at the arboretum. After months of negotiation, the university did an about-face and told us to *get lost* (they weren't that polite). The situation was bizarre.

Fortunately, we had not taken our eye off Tower Hill. On July 2, 1985, the executive committee met with representatives from the Trustees of Reservations to discuss joint ownership of Tower Hill Farm. The preservation of Tower Hill as open space was the primary goal of the organization. If the Horticultural Society was interested in purchasing Tower Hill, TTOR would relinquish their right of first refusal. Phil Beals felt that purchase of the property was doable at no more than $500,000. Also present at the meeting was a quiet elderly lady named Louise Doyle. Soon after we met with Robert Whipple, legal counsel for the Carter estate. Bob was highly regarded by members of the Horticultural Society.

On August 16th, the Executive Committee unanimously approved the acquisition of Tower Hill Farm. Several tasks came out of the meeting: determine the appraisal values of Tower Hill and 30 Elm Street, research agricultural restrictions to lower taxes on Tower Hill, give the trustees a tour of Tower Hill without discussing cost, and begin the fundraising process. 30 Elm Street was appraised for $1,125,000 and Tower Hill for $500,000. Robert Whipple's appraiser had valued the farm at $675,000. We decided not to quibble over the $175,000 differential.

I took trustees individually to see the land and each one was enchanted. At the September 5, 1985 meeting, Cacky Hodgson, a new and young member of the board, moved that we enter into a purchase and sale agreement with the Tower Hill executors. It was voted on and unanimously approved. A swirl of activity commenced. We were confident that the fundraising goal of $2.5 million was reachable and Phil recommended we hire Newtel Associates to manage the campaign. We signed the purchase and sale agreement on October 21, 1985, with a down payment of $3,500 and had a celebratory party on October 23rd in the library at Horticultural Hall. For security purposes we installed Karen, who had recently married Darrell Probst, in the apartment above the garage attached to the old farmhouse. In lieu of rent, they were requested to do minor chores. Closing on the property was set for April 1, 1986.

The first three months of 1986 were a whirlwind of activity. In early January my college mentor Tom Buchter, now Executive Director of the New England Wildflower Society in Framingham, was made chairman of the WCHS Plant Collections Committee along with David Longland, Horticulturist, and Susan Storer, Assistant Horticulturist at the Garden in the Woods. Additional members of the committee were Karen, Darrell and me. We determined it was essential to understand what the collections should be before a single plant was cultured at Tower Hill.

Hines Associates from Boston was hired to evaluate 30 Elm Street and execute a feasibility study of future and potential use. During the two months of study we were not allowed to solicit but could accept offers on the property. The study concluded that, due to the fortress-like construction of the facility, the best reuse of the building was as a museum. The trustees of the Worcester Historical Society were looking for a new location. 30 Elm Street had a grip on their collective imaginations.

We concluded the sale of 30 Elm Street on the first of August. I nervously walked the $1,050,000 check the two blocks for deposit at what was then Shawmut Bank. I remember that I carried a hammer inside my jacket for protection. When I handed the deposit slip and check to the teller, she didn't even raise an eyebrow. The money was booked as board-designated endowment.

I have a thing for numbers. We sold 30 Elm Street, bought 30 Tower Hill Road, and I lived at 30 Cedar Street. Lucky 30! Writing this at the age of sixty-three, it seems lucky still.

John and Frannie

In these early days, I was fortunate to meet many fascinating people, not the least of whom were John and Frannie Herron. They were two of the most enthusiastic supporters of the city of Worcester. When they realized the Horticultural Society was serious about moving their headquarters out of the city where it had been situated for 142 years, they were distressed. Two of Frannie's ancestors were founders of the Horticultural Society. They invited me to dinner at their home on Crown Hill to do a little "lobbying." I arrived at the appointed hour and was immediately offered a martini. I had never had a renowned Herron martini before, but "when in Rome..." One martini led to a second. The conversation was lively and interesting, focusing on Worcester and its

Lively hosts and Worcester ambassadors, John and Frannie Herron

many fine cultural and educational institutions. As I was taking my last sip of my "potent potable," Frannie went to check on dinner. She returned from the kitchen, gave her characteristic laugh and said, "I'm so embarrassed. I forgot to turn on the stove." After several martinis, dinner seemed unimportant. Frannie made delicious sandwiches. I left warmed by the time spent with two such charming people.

A few years after moving to Tower Hill, we received two larger than life bronze herons, a male and a female, from Bob Booth another great supporter of Worcester. Bob was a close friend of the Herrons and, with his permission, we named the statues John and Frannie.

—⁂—

With my encouragement Cush Bozenhard returned to the Horticultural Society as a trustee. He recommended hiring Cullinan Engineering to do a thorough survey of Tower Hill, and also that we have architectural drawings made of the Farmhouse. We learned that the oldest details of the house dated back to the early 1720s.

Right Place, Right Time

Jade Plant

Winona Carter and her husband Maynard, a former executive at the long since defunct Worcester Pressed Steel, had purchased Tower Hill from the Fitzgerald family in 1946. The Fitzgeralds had owned the farm for several generations and, from all reports, the house though stable was run down. The late forties were a time when large historical restoration projects were happening on the east coast, especially at Williamsburg in Virginia and Old Sturbridge Village in Sturbridge, Massachusetts. Mrs. Carter regarded the farmhouse as her own preservation project. She spared no expense in the restoration. Coincidentally, she hired the firm of Dick Brothers to execute the paneling and wainscoting on the first floor, the same firm that had installed the woodwork of the library and director's office at 30 Elm Street.

When we moved in, the only work required was a fresh interior paint job and a refinishing of the floors on the main level. Even though Mrs. Carter had painstakingly restored the house to its eighteenth century original style, her decorating details were Victorian. We removed a fortune in flannel-lined satin drapes from most of the rooms and flocked

Winona Carter's restored jade plant had a place of honor in John's office at Tower Hill. It thrives still in his current home in Westborough, Massachusetts.

wallpaper from the downstairs. The Farmhouse is now an elegant example of eighteenth century architecture.

While in hospice care in late 1983, Mrs. Carter was given a dish garden planted with small common houseplants including a jade plant (*Crassula argentea*). A year and a half later on a tour of the house interior, I noticed the dish garden. All the plants were dead except for a pitiful looking jade plant. I took the dish garden home and nursed the jade plant back to life. It became *Crassula argentea* 'Winona Carter.' I kept that plant in my office for the remainder of my career. When I retired I took a cutting and have it to this day.

—⚏—

The last Society annual meeting was held at Horticulture Hall on January 16th. The gathered members were excited about the acquisition of Tower Hill. As the featured speaker I waxed on, with the help of slides, about the many options we had in building a garden from scratch.

On Saturday, January 25, 1986 in the Chestnut room at 30 Elm Street, we held a facilitated meeting to brainstorm an outline for the new garden as well as educational themes. Board member George Bernardin, Director of Corporate Purchasing and Transportation at Norton Company in Worcester, recommended a facilitator who had worked successfully with the company. The meeting comprised a healthy collection of trustees and interested donors. All ideas were to be entertained and there were no "stupid suggestions." The participants felt free to speak up about what they imagined the garden should represent and the end result was a creative list. In general the ideas fell into three distinct themes: ornamental, economic and ecologic horticulture. The idea was to give the list to a prospective master planner to use as a guide for the general layout of the garden. The most important outcome of the meeting, however, was that everyone was "listened to." They had become part of the process.

That winter, before we actually owned the property, Phil invited photographer Tony King, son-in-law to Helen Stoddard, to come and take black and white photos of the Tower Hill snowscape. The end results were beautiful portraits of the house and barn and the areas immediately adjacent. (See p. 32.)

April 1, 1986 was a very happy Tuesday. Representatives from WCHS met at Bob Whipple's office with a $671,500 check and the Society became owner of the 130-acre Tower Hill Farm.

Darrell and Karen organized the first Tower Hill Plant Sale held on Saturday, May 31 and Darrell was hired as groundskeeper. The plant sale attracted more than a thousand visitors and netted $1,600. It was our first "coming out party."

That spring we selected a landscape architecture firm to execute the Tower Hill Master Plan. I had sent out a request for proposals (RFP) early in the season and received seventeen submissions. The newly organized Master Plan Committee carefully reviewed all the proposals and selected ten firms for interview by the full board. One firm that

Closing on the purchase of Tower Hill Farm, April 1, 1986
Left to right: *Phil Beals, President of WCHS, Brad Bogosian, benefactor of the Carter estate, Robert Florsheim, Vice President of WCHS*

*Geoff Rausch and Melissa (Missy) Marshall
from Environmental Planning and Design, 1986*

was not on our original list was Environmental Planning and Design (EPD), from Pittsburgh. Principal Geoff Rausch asked me why they weren't being considered. I told him that the view of some was that his style was too "cookie cutterish." He assured me that wasn't true, and he would very much appreciate the opportunity to give a presentation. As it turned out, we scheduled five interviews on a Thursday, five on Friday, and Geoffrey's firm the following Monday. The trustees generously gave their time to listen to all the presentations. Our attentive group was astounded when the first ten presenters came to the interview with preconceived ideas of what Tower Hill should look like, without having had a dialog with the Society. Geoffrey came with no set ideas; he was interested in finding out our thoughts. From there the garden design would begin. His one stipulation was to make the building of a maintenance facility our first priority. A formal vote was taken. Of the thirty attendees, twenty-nine voted to hire Environmental Planning and Design. Coincidentally, the one dissenting vote was cast by the same person who did not want me hired as director. A contract was signed with EPD in mid-June, their fee not to exceed $114,245. The process began.

At the same time it was formally decided to enter into a purchase and sale agreement with the Worcester Historical Society's acquisition of the 30 Elm Street property for $1,050,000. The sale was finalized on August 1, 1986.

Geoff Rausch and his associate Melissa Marshall met with us to review the summary from the facilitated meeting we had held in January. They requested any new thoughts we had regarding themes to be represented on the master plan. They were a thoughtful team and we felt comfortable with their style.

With so much going on, we still found time to think about the future of our heritage apple collection. At the time it was planted in a makeshift orchard adjacent to the maintenance building at Old Sturbridge Village. The collection of 119 varieties of apples was gathered in the mid twentieth century by Stearns Lothrop Davenport a renowned "pomologist" and administrator of the Horticultural Society. The first grafted set of trees was grown at Mr. Davenport's farm in North Grafton. In the early 1970s it was decided to re-propagate the collection and move it to Sturbridge. This was done before there was any thought of developing a public garden. The orchard was the first major feature we wanted to include on the master plan. Thanks to the extraordinary grafting skills of Gladys Bozenhard, each variety was carefully grafted onto two different semi-dwarfing rootstocks. This was a Herculean task taken on by Gladys. The young grafted trees were labeled and planted neatly in our nursery in a small field southwest of the farmhouse. Some grafts failed but were quickly re-grafted. The end result was 238 healthy trees.

Gladys Bozenhard pruning one of the heritage apple trees

The Fuller family lived across the street from Tower Hill on Central Street. Russ Fuller regaled me with stories of his youth growing up in Boylston and how Tower Hill Farm had been his playground. He was ecstatic when the Society purchased Tower Hill and he encouraged the Fuller Foundation, which he chaired, to pledge $700,000 to the capital campaign. This pledge alone paid for the property. Wisely, Russ suggested that we host a reception in the Farmhouse for the civic leaders of the town to make them feel a part of the process of development. He knew I would be spending a lot of time meeting with selectmen,

Planning Board, Conservation Committee, Assessors, Boylston Light Department and Highway Department. And indeed I did.

The time had come to give Tower Hill a name and after a thoughtful discussion, the name chosen was Tower Hill Botanic Garden. For historic reasons everyone agreed to keep the name Tower Hill. By using the epithet Botanic Garden, we were letting people know the seriousness of our educational mission.

But why did we choose *Botanic* Garden and not *Botanical* Garden? At the time I was a great admirer of the Brooklyn Botanic Garden, a garden worth emulating, but not the New York Botanical Garden, a garden in poor repair and floundering. The tides have now turned and the New York Botanical Garden is now a gloriously beautiful public garden as is the Brooklyn Botanic Garden.

Tower Hill's first entrance sign on Route 70, designed by Bob Zeleniak, 1986

The staff at the entrance of Tower Hill Botanic Garden, 1992
Front row, left to right: *Arthur Brooks, Ginny Rich, Kevin Smola, Margot Wallin, Karen Perkins, Pat DuFosse.* Second Row: *Joann Vieira, John Trexler, Debi Hogan, John Mapel, Joanne Martin*

―― CHAPTER FIVE ――

From the Inside Out

Tower Hill Origin

In the early 1890s, the farm was labeled Tower Hill when the highest area on the property was used as a triangulation point during the survey for the creation of the Wachusett Reservoir. A tower was erected to enable the surveyors to see the breadth of the Nassau River, which would be dammed to create the reservoir. Before that, the area shared a name with neighboring Faggot Hill.

Once the property was officially named Tower Hill Botanic Garden, it was time to review our mission and establish solid objectives. The committee selected for this purpose came up with the following:

> Mission and Objectives:
>
> As stated in the Society's Charter adopted March 3, 1842 and readopted November 20, 1986, the Society exists as an educational organization "for the purpose of advancing the science and encouraging and improving the practice of horticulture."

Above: Mountain silverbell (*Halesia tetraptera* var. *monticola*)

The Society shall fulfill this purpose by pursuing the following objectives:

1. To establish a botanic garden of the highest educational and aesthetic quality at Tower Hill, displaying superior woody and herbaceous plants suited to New England conditions, and to develop, test, introduce, and disseminate selected varieties.

2. To develop and maintain the proper facilities necessary to keep the garden open to the public.

3. To provide educational services to the public, students, and professionals in the field of horticulture and related subjects.

4. To maintain a library that is open to the public and consistent with the objectives of the Society.

5. To provide scholarships and recognition for students of horticulture and to give awards for horticultural excellence to gardeners and exhibitors.

6. To promote appreciation for horticulture in its relationship to wildlife, ecology, and other aspects of the natural environment.

7. To provide services requiring horticultural or botanical expertise to public and private institutions.

8. To cooperate with horticultural and botanical institutions, plant societies, and related organizations.

The objectives were used as a framework for the development of the Master Plan.

We had promised ourselves to be patient and wait for the master planning process to be complete before we put a shovel in the ground and planted a single plant. We did, however, remove a few plants such as the two large yews to either side of the front door of the Farmhouse and some miscellaneous rhododendrons acting as foundation plants along the south wall of the dairy barn. We also decided to install a small garden nestled in the southeast facing "L" of the Farmhouse and garage.

From the Inside Out

Darrell Probst had proven to be a talented plantsman and was given the task of laying out the design. I gave him boundaries and axis points to work with. The two axis points were the center of the east-facing window of what was then my office in the Farmhouse and the center of the south-facing tool shed door at the southeast corner of the garage. The boundaries were the east façade of the Farmhouse, the south façade of the garage, a large sugar maple south and slightly east of the Farmhouse, an old lamppost southeast of the garage, and a curved contour, a remnant of an old nineteenth-century road that passed in front of the Farmhouse. Darrell worked with these details and created a charming garden. The garden proved so successful, it became a part of the Master Plan and was named the Cottage Garden. Darrell also laid out a vegetable garden where the Carters had had a small vegetable patch. The design was controlled by the east axis of the director's office window and the curved contour.

A view of the Cottage Garden, 2011

The Tower Hill Mantra

As the curious found their way up Tower Hill Road, I began to give regular tours. With the Cottage Garden looking so good, it was easy to wax poetic about two simple rules:

1. Arrange plants from the inside out, a garden composition is primarily admired from various windows of the house. You spend most of your time indoors, make sure your garden gives you pleasure from the inside out.

2. Plant for winter first and all other seasons second. Winter in New England is not three months long; it's more like six months long. Make sure the plants you select have strong winter interest. It's easy to be seduced by spring flowering trees and shrubs but how they look in the winter is paramount.

Tax Exempt Status

Under the Horticultural Society's umbrella, we assumed we would be exempt from real estate taxes. However, the legal council for Boylston informed us that according to state law we were not. The convoluted story goes back to the 1930s when WCHS "innocently" failed to pay taxes to the city of Worcester on income made from the lease of the property on Front Street. There was actually no law on the books stating that non-related income of horticultural societies was taxable. But there soon was. The state legislature passed a law stating that any real-estate not directly supporting the educational mission of a horticultural society would be taxed. The town arbitrarily ruled that all buildings at Tower Hill and fifteen acres of land would be tax exempt, the remaining acreage to be taxed at an agricultural rate. We made the argument that all of Tower Hill was a botanic garden and was used to support our mission but they wouldn't relent. As we made trails and developed more of the acreage, we argued that our tax-exempt acreage should be enlarged, but to no avail. The trustees eventually agreed that the relatively small amount was worth paying in order to maintain good relations with the town. The topic is still brought up and debated internally.

After the Farmhouse was renovated in mid-July, we began moving in. We were ready to open to the public on Monday, August 4, 1986—coincidentally also the twenty-fourth anniversary of Marilyn Monroe's death. The circulating collection of the library miraculously fit into the southeast parlor, on shelves purchased at a now defunct store called Conran's. The librarian was set up at a small desk in the corner by the fireplace. The receptionist/membership secretary was situated in the southwest parlor. The north room was used for trustee meetings and as a classroom. Karen's and my office were upstairs. Most of the formal furnishings from the director's office at Elm Street fit neatly into my office, once the master bedroom. It felt right to establish some of the interior history in the new location: the director's desk, Harry Stoddard's pentagonal table and painted Italian cabinet, Bernice Heald's floor lamp with mica shade and gilded mirror, beautiful rugs left behind after the sale, and various knick-knacks given by a variety of members, some of which were Winona Carter's.

Darrell set up the maintenance equipment in the three-bay garage: our sturdy twenty-one-inch Honda lawn mower, rakes, shovels, pole pruners, hoses and watering cans. That first day members and others made their way up the hill to wish us well and wander around. Many of the non-members were inspired by the vision and direction that the Society was embarking on and the membership began to grow. We were two years from completing the Master Plan but the most frequent comment from visitors was, "You must be very excited by what is happening." I was, but mainly I thought about all the detailed work we had already done and all the work that was yet to be accomplished. We had to keep the momentum in order to reach our goals.

TORNADO

On August 7th, three days after we opened, the sky turned a strange and angry color. Winds increased exponentially by the moment. The maple trees in front of the Farmhouse whipped back and forth. Darrell was convinced we were about to experience a tornado and we decided that the basement was the wisest place to sit out the storm. The winds sounded like the roar of a freight train and then stopped all at once. We went upstairs dreading the destruction that would surely greet us. Amazingly, the house was completely intact and there was barely a leaf or branch on the ground. Darrell and I were still convinced that a tornado had passed through. As we walked in the direction of the Tower Hill summit, we saw dozens of trees that had been snapped in two, leaving a tangled mess of trunks and branches. Within a few days, however, we had the debris cleaned up.

The damaged area would become the future location of the septic field and the Belvedere. Mother Nature had done our tree removal work.

The Grand Duchess

During the early years of Tower Hill, I often worked at my desk after the property closed and the staff had gone home. One evening the phone rang, and I picked up with my standard greeting, "Tower Hill Botanic Garden, how may I help you?" I was answered with an exasperated sigh.

"Who am I talking to?" the caller demanded.

"John Trexler, the Executive Director," I replied with what I hoped was an authoritarian tone.

It became clear the woman was articulate but confused. She told me about her former life in Russia, how her father was in the cabinet of Tsar Nicholas II, how Grand Duchess Anastasia was her playmate, and how her family lost millions of dollars and acres of land when the communists took power. Her family came to America penniless. Gradually her father had gotten back on his feet, made another fortune and acquired thousands of acres only to lose everything again. Tower Hill, she claimed, had been his.

I sympathized and gently ended the conversation, scratching my head. I figured this was the end of my connection with this sad and deluded "Grand Duchess." However, she called several other times during regular working hours. I listened but told her that her father could not have owned Tower Hill. She didn't take this well.

One day as I made my way to my car to go home, the "Grand Duchess" was there in the parking lot waiting to confront me. She made threats and demanded that Tower Hill be returned. It was clear she had been drinking. When I told her to leave and not bother me anymore, she got into her wreck of a car and slowly drove off. I ran back to the office, called the police, gave them a description of the car and suggested they have a chat with the woman. A bit later the police called back. They had explained my concerns to the Duchess and informed her that she was not to contact me in the future. It worked. She never bothered me again.

Working Paper

Before beginning the physical plan of the gardens, Geoff Rausch and Melissa Marshall created a "Working Paper" that touched upon several important topics. The paper is included in the appendix of this book.

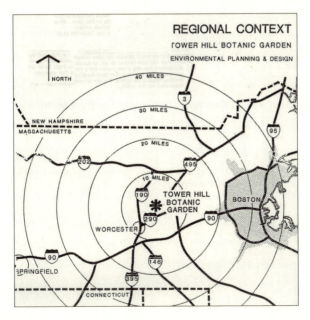

An illustration from the Working Paper placing Tower Hill in regional context

Geoff Rausch agreed to be the speaker for the 1987 annual meeting in January. He regaled the membership with his vision for the master planning process.

A few weeks after the talk, Geoff made an observation and a determination. The main entry to the botanic garden could not be Tower Hill Road off Route 70, due to poor site distance. It had to branch off French Drive, a road perpendicular to Route 70. There was one problem. We didn't own the two-acre, pie-shaped parcel the road would transverse. He suggested we acquire it.

It was clear that Russ Fuller was the "go to" guy in Boylston. I gave Russ a call to inquire about the land parcel. It belonged to a "very nice woman" named Janet Bradford and Russ gave me her phone number. Janet answered my call on the second ring. She knew why I was calling —Russ had already informed her.

"You'd like to buy that parcel I own on French Drive?"

"Yes," I said.

"Well, I would be happy to sell it to you," was her quick reply.

Two weeks and $35,000 later we owned a good piece of frontage on French Drive. The garden entrance had been established. A major feature of the master plan was determined. We were on our way.

—⚘—

In order to introduce building mass into the planning process, Geoff received input from a Pittsburgh-based architect. Our reaction was that, if an architect's advice was needed, the architect should be from New England.

The process of identifying an architect was similar to hiring a master planner. We sent out an RFP, received twenty responses and agreed to interview ten. Yet again, nine of the firms came with preconceived ideas of what the building(s) should look like. One firm waxed poetic about a gleaming white porcelain structure commanding the hill. We were not impressed—in fact, we were horrified. The firm of Juster, Pope, Frazier (JPF), from Shelburne Falls, Massachusetts, came to the interview with no preconceptions. They wanted ideas from us as well as the master

From the Inside Out

Left to right: *John Trexler, Norton Juster, Earl Pope, Geoff Rausch, 1991*

planners. Designing is a creative process and it requires thoughtful input from both the owners and the people who are actually going to use the facility. Geoff, JPF and WCHS had similar visions for the process.

JPF first considered the new building as an extension of the Farmhouse, either on an east-west axis or a north-south axis. It was decided that the Farmhouse should stand alone. The new building would be located northwest of the Farmhouse, "off slope" of the level spine of the hill with a view of the reservoir and Mt. Wachusett.

"Not so fast" goes the old adage. Geoff reminded us that we had not determined the location of a leaching field for the septic system. The leaching field had to accommodate the full occupancy of the building, both present and future. An engineer examined the soils by performing percolation tests. Some tests were done in the areas that are now the Inner Park and Shade Garden and the open fields. All of these locations were down slope of the proposed building in order for the field to be gravity fed. Dozens of areas were tested none of them yielding positive results. This was, needless to say, distressing. We then started looking up slope from the proposed building site, starting with an area south of the rise to the Tower Hill summit.

It was raining the morning of this particular test. The field was too wet for the truck carrying the equipment to transverse. Buckets of water and shovels had to be walked the distance across the west field to the location. A lighter backhoe was able to drive the distance. Present were a representative from the Boylston conservation commission, a member of the Board of Health, the engineer, Geoff Rausch and me. The backhoe operator dug a hole the prescribed depth and then another cylindrical hole with a diameter of eighteen inches and a depth of twelve inches. We began the percolation test by pouring water into the tidy hole and discovered that more water was needed. Like a terrified prospective father, I walked the width of the muddy field to tap the hydrant on Tower Hill road for more water. When the last of the water was poured, we looked at our watches to see how quickly the water would "perc." It went amazingly fast. We had found the location for the leaching field, albeit up hill from the proposed building.

Geoff framed a photo of the perc hole and titled it "The Hole That Made It All Possible."

The core of the building complex began to take shape but not before Geoff started developing a "bubble diagram." Shapes were drawn and placed on a contour plan of the property in relationship to the core buildings. Each bubble was labeled a landscape "type." Bubbles could change shape and squeeze between one another until they were in a location we liked and in the right relationship to an adjacent bubble. Geoff arranged the first diagram in a way he thought made sense and for the most part we agreed. The one exception was the bubble representing the Rock Garden. The majority felt its relationship with the east slope of the Tower Hill summit was too invasive to an area we felt should be left alone. The Rock Garden bubble moved to a rocky rise adjacent to one labeled "Shade Garden." With this diagram approved, Geoff put pen to paper and began showing the actual proposed boundaries of buildings and landscape.

The building complex was planned to be a quadrangle with the Education and Visitors Center to the west, an Orangerie northeast of the Center, an enclosed walkway southeast and a complex of conservatories and a restaurant to the east. In the middle of the quad would be an open Winter Garden with a central pool. The control axis of the quadrangle was off the central arch of the Farmhouse's back porch.

The Visitors Center became 265 feet long and 55 feet wide. A twelve-foot-wide gallery ran along the east side with points of egress at the north and south ends. An allée of oak trees was designed to be on axis with the north door of the Visitors Center, the allée being 300 feet long with ten pairs of varying oak species (*Quercicum*) and terminating on a fountain and bench. On axis and to the north of the Orangerie would be a rose garden and a perennial garden separated by a panel of grass on the central east-west axis of the oak allée. A container court and garden for the physically challenged was to be situated south and on axis to the enclosed walkway and Farmhouse. The Lawn Garden and Secret Garden would be located south of the Farmhouse and on axis with the front door. South of the Secret Garden and on axis would be the southwest field of the apple orchard and beyond that the native forest.

Planning the ornamental gardens on a strict north-south axis on the flats of the hill was more than just classic compass control. It was also a way for the gardens to be subordinate to the fields and orchard. The plantings to the east and west of the gardens would be primarily indigenous species of trees and shrubs to compliment the edges of the fields and meadows. Being authentic to the rural quality of the property was paramount. Our love affair with Tower Hill began when we first saw the natural beauty of the open and forested areas. After setting eyes on Tower Hill for the first time, renowned horticulturist and garden designer Gary Koller said it all, "Don't touch it, it's perfect as is."

Our job was definitely to touch it—but with care and respect for the integrity of the property.

Once the complex of buildings was sited and the agreed-upon themes of the ornamental gardens were arranged on the main axis, the "economic" gardens were determined. From north to south they were: a Medicinal Garden, Herb Garden, Vegetable Garden, Nut Grove, Fruit Garden and Orchard. All these landscapes were sited within the boundaries of existing fields.

Moving east, the "ecologic" gardens fell into place. Again, from north to south, were planned: the Flower Walk, Field, Meadow, Wildlife Garden, Shade Garden, Rock Garden, and Dry Garden. The hundred plus acres of woods and untouched fields were meant to be protective buffers—never to be developed.

There were two proposed landscapes and a building complex that had no direct relationship with the central axis of the garden. They were: the Pinetum (a collection of conifers), the Children's Garden (a farm in miniature to reflect the agrarian heritage of Tower Hill), the Maintenance Barn, horticulture offices and the Plant Nursery.

Geoff stood by what he pronounced at his interview. "The first building you will construct is a maintenance building." Sure enough, one of the bubbles was prominently labeled "Maintenance Facility." It was tucked in an existing field southeast of the Apple Orchard and beyond the far end of the parking lots. The facility would need its own septic system. Fortunately, it was a comparatively painless task to find a leaching field west and down-slope of the proposed buildings and the Children's Garden.

A suggestion was made to consider a Morton Building as our Maintenance Barn. After reviewing specifications and seeing such a building on the Boylston property of Bigelow Nurseries, we all agreed it was the right design for the site. However, rather than have the customary metal siding, we went with cedar. The dimensions were determined by thinking long and hard on what our ultimate needs would be. Geoff sited the barn on the plan with our dimensions—yet another important goal met. We erected the Maintenance Barn in the summer of 1988. At the same time we hired an architect to design the conversion of the three-bay garage for the Farmhouse into a meeting/classroom,

From the Inside Out

The Maintenance Barn under construction, 1988

and what had been the kitchen for the apartment into two restrooms, one handicapped accessible.

All of this activity made it clear that we had to tap into the town water line at the base of Tower Hill Road. The water main was installed in the summer of 1988. Both the Farmhouse and Maintenance Barn benefited from this addition.

By the time the Master Plan (see version on p. 97) was unveiled on September 19, 1988, we had the beginnings of a trail system, a Maintenance Barn complete with office and bathroom, the Cottage and Vegetable Gardens, and the Farmhouse meeting room.

Four hundred attended the unveiling, nearly fifty percent of the membership. The event took place under a tent on the front lawn of the Farmhouse. The plan was attached to a makeshift frame and placed at the east end of the tent. Geoff Rausch, Phil Beals and I gave short congratulatory speeches. Everyone was enthralled, though a few were skeptical of what was described as a fifty-year plan. Most everyone attending—including yours truly—might be dead by 2038.

The glow of the unveiling was still fresh when we began discussing the details of the Lawn Garden and the purchase of a half-acre parcel on Tower Hill Road.

It was unanimously decided by late summer 1988, that the first phase of development for Tower Hill would be the Lawn Garden. Initially, we presumed the Education and Visitors Center would be a priority but it fell second on the shortlist of immediate goals. The Lawn Garden would give us two essential features: an outstanding collection of ornamental trees, shrubs, and vines and a large open space for outdoor events. Geoff was hired to design-out the details of the garden rendered on the Master Plan.

The acquisition of the two remaining properties with frontage on Tower Hill Road was also essential. This would give us full control of the road, enabling us to use it as a service entrance, an alternate exit during high visitation events and for emergencies. It might be years before this was accomplished but that's what master planning is all about.

Working on the design details of the Lawn Garden was great fun. As the process went along, the board of trustees had opportunities to review and comment. The overall layout fit neatly between two hedgerows of trees and the former apple and pear orchards. In order for it to work with the existing grades, the garden had three distinct levels: the

Details of Lawn Garden elevation drawings, 1988

upper terrace adjacent to the Farmhouse granite curb, the 300-feet-long lawn panel which gradually descended to an overlook flanked by twin pergolas, and an area seven feet below the overlook accessed by twin curving staircases which framed a half-moon pool. This lower area was the Secret Garden—so named because you couldn't see it from the front door of the Farmhouse. It only came into view once you reached the overlook at the end of the lawn panel.

The first stab at the pergolas and staircase was quite different from the end result. Geoff and his partner Missy Marshall designed one large pergola that stretched across the overlook and a very broad staircase that descended on axis to the Secret Garden. They had forgotten to include a wheelchair accessible path from the lawn panel to the Secret Garden. Cacky Hodgson pointed out this oversight. It was seamlessly integrated along the eastern border. Design lessons from Skylands led me to suggest the twin stairs and pergolas and the half-moon pool.

The primary hardscape consisted of an elaborate series of brick and bluestone paths. The three-foot wide bluestone path framed the oval lawn of the Secret Garden acting as a viewing path for the herbaceous and shrub borders. The main brick paths made a 360-degree broad hourglass system for exploring the extensive collection of trees and shrubs and a serpentine brick path led down to the Secret Garden. The chosen brick was sand cast and arranged in a herringbone pattern. Sand cast bricks are irregular and this made the path look weathered. The bricks are difficult to lay because they make irregular seams but we wanted to emulate the look of old weathered brick paths. Some folks were critical of this but they eventually understood.

On the finished plan, Geoff and Missy showed massings of deciduous and evergreen trees and shrubs. It was our responsibility to select the plants for these locations. The collective knowledge and experience of the Plant Collections Committee in making a list of plants was essential and Joann Wright (Vieira) and I partnered to pull it all together.

A single specimen tree was sited at the southwest end of the lawn on the detailed plan of the Lawn Garden. The icon indicated a deciduous tree with a mature spread of sixty feet. One early spring day Karen,

Darrell, Joann and I took a trip to the Arnold Arboretum to identify a species that would be optimal for that location. Many of the specimens at the arboretum were more than a hundred years old, a good time frame from which to make our selection. Our criterion was a tree that had four seasons of interest. The tree that caught our eye was a Korean mountain ash (*Sorbus alnifolia*). We paced the drip line of the tree and determined that the specimen was approximately sixty feet in diameter. The small red fruit from the year before was still conspicuous, the silhouette majestic, and we knew it would be covered in white spring bloom with a burnt orange tinge to the leaves in autumn—the perfect tree. It was susceptible to diseases common to trees in the rose family but worth the risk. We had done our due diligence.

Early in my career I learned that it's best to plant trees or shrubs when they are small. They establish more quickly and, in a couple of years, catch up to larger, more expensive plants. A thousand plus or minus plants were sited, installed and generously mulched with woodchips obtained from clearing the Lawn Garden site and the three acres of the proposed meadow garden. The unanimous opinion was that the garden looked like a skin of mulch with small green blemishes. Patience, however, is a virtue, especially in the garden, and we were very virtuous. By the fifth growing season the plantings had knitted together and looked healthy and established.

There are, of course, exceptions to every rule. In April 1988 we were given beautiful specimens of stewartia (*Stewartia pseudocamellia*) and umbrella pine (*Sciadopytis verticillata*), the latter from Robert Bunting of Holden and the former from the retired Cary Nursery on Route 9 in Shrewsbury.

Mr. Bunting had bought the umbrella pine from Bigelow Nurseries in Northborough and was told it was a small slow-growing tree. He planted it in front of his living room picture window only to learn that it was not slow-growing, nor was it small. He decided to give a gift to Tower Hill in memory of his wife Dorothy and, at the same time, recover the view from his window. The original plan was to move the tree in autumn of 1987, but Jim Foster, who had been awarded the job,

The Lawn Garden, 1988

discovered that the tree was growing on top of a very large boulder. He halted the operation and informed us that he would be more comfortable finishing the move the following spring.

In early April, Jim and his crew dug what turned out to be a very flat lopsided oval of a root mass, about six feet long, four feet wide, and eighteen inches deep. The tree was hoisted onto the back of a flatbed truck and driven slowly to Tower Hill. Darrell had dug a hole to accommodate the "odd ball," the site just to the right of the southeast corner of the Farmhouse. The tree fit comfortably into the hole and was watered/mudded into place and staked and generously mulched with woodchips. The tree took hold and put on very healthy new growth. It never skipped a beat.

The landscape crew from Bigelow Nurseries skillfully dug the stewartia, a healthy forty-year-old tree. The ball was at least nine feet in diameter and six feet in depth. It was carefully transported to Tower

Planting the umbrella pine, 1988

Hill, gently placed in an oversized hole and generously watered and mulched. In contrast to the umbrella pine, it never took hold and died after five years.

Both trees were dedicated on Arbor Day weekend 1988, four-and-a-half months before the unveiling of the Master Plan.

From the Inside Out

Ed Cary, nurseryman and benefactor of Tower Hill, with the Cary Award ribbon. The Society established the Cary Award progam to identify woody plant selections to introduce home gardeners to ideal plants for New England gardens.

CARY AWARD

Ed Cary and his brother owned the Cary Brothers Nursery on Route 9 in Shrewsbury. He bequeathed a quarter of his estate amounting to $210,000 (and the stewartia) to the Horticultural Society. Half the bequest was for the support of the library, the other half for prizes in horticulture.

While working in New Jersey, I had served on the Gold Medal Committee of the Pennsylvania Horticultural Society. The Gold Medal identified outstanding plants for a region spanning from New York City to Washington, D.C. From the moment I moved to Worcester, I thought that it would be useful for New England gardeners to have a similar program for the six New England states. The gift of the Cary endowment made this possible. A committee comprised of nursery owners and horticulturists from New England developed the criteria and inaugurated the Cary Award program in 1997. Our goal was to make the public aware of outstanding trees, shrubs, and vines with multi-seasonal interest. We selected plants that were readily available in the nursery trade and gave nursery owners plenty of lead-time for propagation. The 1997 selections were: *Chamaecyparis* (now *Xanthocyparis*) *nootkatensis* 'Pendula', *Enkianthus campanulatus, Fothergilla major, Magnolia kobus* 'Centennial', and *Stewartia pseudocamellia.* The program has been successful in disseminating outstanding woody plants to the gardening public. Michael Arnum, Marketing Director at Tower Hill for nineteen years, deserves most of the credit for the success of the program. He also developed a comprehensive marketing plan for WCHS which greatly expanded visitation and reach at Tower Hill. He successfully spearheaded and managed our original website with the creative and technical assistance of Ingrid Mach and Bob Zeleniak.

Michael Arnum at Tower Hill, 1993

From the Inside Out

SUSAN DUMAINE

An influential member of the Cary Award Committee was Susan Dumaine from Weston, Massachusetts. There was no individual more involved with the evolution of Tower Hill. In the early years, she served on the Regional Gardens Committee, a group that included representatives from the Arnold Arboretum, Massachusetts Horicultural Society, Mt. Auburn Cemetery, New England Wildflower Society, and WCHS. Susan was involved with all these institutions. She was on the Plant Collections Committee and Education Committee where she helped organize the New England School of Gardening at Tower Hill, The Cary Award Committee, the WCHS Board of Trustees, and the Executive Committee. Her involvement only stopped when she and her husband Dudley sold their beautiful home and garden and moved to Kentucky to be closer to their daughter.

Susan had an antique ruby ring that I admired. Before moving to Kentucky she wrote me a letter and said she had bequeathed it to WCHS. A few months before she died in February 2012, she wrote me another letter to say that she had changed her mind. The ring was going to her daughter. Enclosed in the envelope was a check for $25,000 for the "educational goals of the Society."

Susan Dumaine, educator extraordinaire

As if I wasn't busy enough, I got it in my head to do an updated rewrite of Arabella Tucker's 1894 book, *Trees of Worcester*. Arabella had been a professor at the Worcester Normal School (now Worcester State University) and she had a great love of the Worcester urban forest. I thought an update would be easy—bad word, *easy*. I gave myself a publish date of March, 1992, the 150th anniversary of WCHS. I did not meet the deadline. I ended up hiring Evelyn Herwitz, a journalist from Worcester, to write the book with financial support from the Nathaniel Wheeler Trust. The new goal was 1994, the 100th anniversary of Tucker's original book. That goal was not met. It was published in 2001, a good start to the new millennium. With such a slow pace the book was easy enough to work on. In the interim, I was focused on the planting of the Orchard, grading and paving the entrance drive, grading the parking lots, as well as Phase II and Phase III of the Master Plan.

In July of 1988, I recommended the hiring of Joann Wright as a full time gardener. Joann had proven to be a stellar intern. She was meticulous, focused, and quick to learn—her energy infectious. She was raised to the position of Superintendent of Horticulture in 1989 after Darrell left to start a nursery business.

Joann's and my first major project together was the laying out and planting of the heritage apple collection. Once we were sure that the grafts done by Gladys Bozenhard had taken, the young trees were planted in the nursery adjacent to the new barn. The trees were fertilized, well watered, and given the appropriate fungicidal treatment. By the fourth growing season in spring 1990, the trees were ready to be planted in their permanent home. The heritage collection was to be located in two of the four fields addressed by the Master Plan: the large field parallel to the Lawn Garden and the field southeast of the barn. There were a total of 238 trees. We divided the trees into three groups of ripening seasons, early (late August, early September), mid (late September, early November), and late (late November, early December). The largest group was the late season trees. We determined they would fit in the field adjacent to the barn. The early and mid season would be planted in the field parallel to the Lawn Garden. Dividing these two

John and Joann (Wright) Vieira planting the heritage apple collection, 1990

fields was the entrance drive, our control point. Following the curve of the drive, we measured a comfortable distance from where we knew the pavement would end and from the drainage swale. The stakes were spaced eighteen feet apart in a row and twenty-two feet between rows. We also had to take into consideration the eastern shrub border of the Lawn Garden to the west and the loop trail to the east. With tape measure in hands, Joann and I carefully placed the stakes marking the center of where the holes would be dug. Maybe because of the precision of our work, we became very silly, shouting out the name "Watteau" (an eighteenth-century French artist) every time a stake went in. To this day Joann and I laugh every time we think back to those days of laying out the orchard.

With the 238 stakes in the ground, it was time to dig the holes. A member of the Lauring construction crew working on the Lawn Garden volunteered as backhoe operator (thanks to Joann batting her beautiful eyelashes). The holes were dug in late November, early December 1989. We were careful to place the stakes back in the centers of the holes. The soil was augmented with good organic matter. We were prepared to plant the following spring. On April 7, 1990, Joann, eight volunteers and I planted 160 trees. With the assistance of Duke Dawson, my job was to dig the trees bare-root from the nursery and place them in a barrel of water. They were then taken to the field and planted in their coinciding hole. Another fifteen trees were planted a few days later. The remaining trees were planted spring of 1991. Watteau!

Decoupage, Décolletage, and Jews

At a party hosted by Helen Stoddard to celebrate the publishing of Ken Druse's *The Natural Garden*, a book that featured a beautiful full-page picture of the famous Moss Steps in her garden, I was witnessed to two amusing incidences. I was seated at a table with Barbara Booth and a well-known man who will remain nameless. Barbara was wearing a beautiful black cocktail dress with a V-neck, accessorized with a substantial gold brooch. The man stared at Barbara's neckline inappropriately and then announced, "Mrs. Booth, I love your *decoupage.*"

Barbara's eyes widened for a moment and then she coolly responded, "I think you're attempting to say *décolletage.*" After a brief uncomfortable silence, we proceeded with dinner.

Afterward, while we enjoyed our coffee in another room a guest cornered me and asked, "John, is Mr. Druse Jewish?" Stunned by the question, I simply said "yes." Those were the days.

From the Inside Out

Intrepid volunteers planted thousands of daffodil bulbs in 1989. The fruits of their labors are evident in this photo from 1994.

In October of 1989 I felt a good and "simple" project would be to plant daffodil bulbs in the field garden. Joann and I decided on six thousand bulbs of five different naturalizing varieties. An army of sixty volunteers with shovels in hand were tapped to make short work of the project. Sure enough the bulbs went in and in record time. Little did we know that beneath the field was a mass of poison ivy roots. A few days after the planting we started getting reports from the volunteers that they had contracted poison ivy. Approximately half the volunteers were infected and they were not happy. Board member and volunteer, George Bernardin, wrote a poem to mark the occasion "Daffy Digger's Lament." It goes as follows:

> It was a clear and cool October day
> When we came to for no pay
> To Boylston Town's Tower Hill

We came to plant daffodils
In vast numbers to create spring glory
And thus proclaim the WCHS Story
Ginny, in the house made muffins and soup
To nourish the motley volunteer troop
Thousands of bulbs were planted real well
Young and old felt tired but swell
All went home for baths and booze
And some are suspected of sneaking a snooze.
A success we thought, but there was a hitch,
Because next day, began the itch.
The itch, the itch, the itch, the itch
That was the hitch that was the bitch.
It seems that John had a fiendish plot
To have us clear a lethal lot
The field, in fact, was a massive mine
Of poison ivy, its roots and vine.
After many days the rashes did finally heal
We conjured great ways for John's fate to seal.
Now the planting work is done
The bulbs await the April sun.
But when we view that springtime splendor
Some of us will feel, an itch, an itch, an itch.

One of my earliest Worcester introductions was to Frank and Louise Harrington. Frank was the retired president and founder of Paul Revere Insurance Company in Worcester. Louise was the sister of Dorothy Hurlburt, wife of Waite Hurlburt, past president of the Horticultural Society and retired president of Peoples Bank. Louise loved gardening and Frank was enamored with fruit trees. We became friends and I was a frequent visitor to their home on William Street. On one visit I decided to test Frank's knowledge of fruit. I brought a quince that looked identical to a ripe pear. I stood in the threshold of the library with Frank at the far end, held up the fruit and said, "What is this?"

Without hesitation, Frank replied, "Quince."

Frank was generous. In honor of his wife Louise he supported the annual maintenance of the garden at Horticultural Hall on Chestnut

Street. Later he made a $20,000 endowment gift in memory of his brother-in-law Waite Hurlburt for the care of the gardens at Tower Hill. When Frank died in the late 80s, Louise and his four children gave $25,000 each for the creation of an endowment in Frank's memory to support the maintenance of the orchard at Tower Hill. The orchard was officially named the "Frank L. Harrington, Sr. Orchard." This came about at the same time Joann and I were planting the apple trees.

Shortly before Frank died, I arranged for Gladys Bozenhard to graft a few scions from our historic collection onto Frank's espaliered apple tree that grew up the back wall of his home. He sat in a chair mesmerized and watched as Gladys worked her magic.

The Harrington gift triggered two other major gifts in support of the Lawn Garden. John Jeppson, retired CEO of Norton Company, gave $50,000 to name the upper terrace in memory of his mother Selma

Ceremony for the Lawn Garden, 1989
Left to right: *John Trexler, Helen Stoddard, Bob Booth, Phil Beals, Hope Spear*

Ulrika Jeppson. John and his wife Marianne maintained a home in Worcester and a magnificent farm in Brookfield, Massachusetts. They had a great respect for the Tower Hill Master Plan.

Phil Beals, the recently retired president of the Horticultural Society and founding president of Tower Hill, made a $100,000 gift to name the Secret Garden in memory of his mother Edith. He owned a farm as well in Southborough.

The Lawn Garden and Orchard were dedicated at a gala party on September 16, 1990. In the 1990 Transactions, I summarized the Lawn Garden:

> The Lawn Garden began in 1989 with the rough grading of its contours. This served as a springboard for the flurry of construction that took place in 1990. Tens of thousands of bricks were laid along hundreds of feet of path. Hundreds of tons of bluestone were set into place as caps on walls and paving of terraces. Dozens of truckloads of stone made their way from Hardwick to be skillfully incorporated into several hundred cubic yards of beautiful wall. Many board feet of western red cedar made their way from Colorado to a wood working shop in Worcester to be crafted into two matching pergolas, each twenty-two feet long, seventeen feet wide and eleven feet tall. Several cubic feet of concrete got poured to form the half-moon shaped pool and two flanking curved stairways that descend seven feet from the pergolas to the pool and Secret Garden. Hundreds of cubic yards of mixed topsoil were graded to create level lawns and bermed beds. Lastly, one thousand plants representing 350 species and cultivars of ornamental trees and shrubs got planted in fourteen beds that frame the panel of grass.

The development of Tower Hill into a botanic garden was a series of overlapping efforts: projects in the design stage, projects in the preparation stage, projects in construction, and projects dedicated.

The entrance drive was built in 1991. As was my method and madness, I walked the proposed route many times until I felt comfortable with what Geoffrey had proposed. I put marking tape around trees that stood where the center of the paving would be. I organized walking tours

From the Inside Out

Fuller Drive flanked by the Frank L. Harrington, Sr., Orchard, 2013

with trustees and donors so that they too could envision the finished product. In early spring, we hired the Westborough-based engineering company Beals (no relation to Phil) and Thomas to survey and produce engineered working drawings. Bids went out to several construction contractors who specialized in roads. With Cush Bozenhard's encouragement, we hired Marois Brothers whose lead foreman was Norman (Happy) Benoit.

First on site were enormous tree-removal machines that could cut through a whole tree and guide it through a chipper—impressive and frightening. Stumps were removed and grading equipment began defining the broad trail. The rest followed quickly—gravel, dense grade, and compaction. Swales were formed to take away storm water and melting snow. Even without macadam the drive looked settled.

The drawings showed a low wall on the west side of the entrance from French Drive. Happy and I had a powwow and concluded there should be a matching wall on the east side for balance as well as a set

The Fuller family standing on the center-line of Fuller Drive, 1991
Left to right: *Joyce, Mark, Ernest, Russ*

of pillars for scale and for the support of a gate. I never considered that this extra work was not budgeted. I just held my breath and hoped no one would notice when the invoices came in. No one did. The paving was finally installed, and voilà, we had an entrance drive. The primary financial support for the road came from the Fuller Foundation which entitled them to the naming rights. The road was formally christened the "George F. and Sybil H. Fuller Drive" on September 14, 1991. There was a ribbon-cutting and a parade of antique cars before the attendees drove their cars up the hill for a reception in the Farmhouse.

The story of the "what ifs" must be told. Dealing with conservation commissions has its challenges. Even though the plans for the drive had been approved by the Boylston Conservation Commission, they came to us mid-construction and required us to install a retention pond on the east side of the entrance. Their argument was, *"What if* a bus starts its ascent up the hill and the transmission falls out, and *what if* transmission fluid and oil pours onto the pavement, and *what if* there's an unexpected downpour of rain that washes these pollutants into the brook with no name that parallels and goes under French Drive and ultimately flows to the Wachusett Reservoir. A detention pond was essential to save the day.

The following spring, John Jeppson offered some Catawba rhododendrons that he had grown from seed. Never one to say "no," I accepted. Joann took the truck out to Oakholm, the Jeppson farm in Brookfield, dug the two-foot plants from a small nursery and brought them back to Tower Hill. They were planted in the woods that bordered Fuller Drive—some survived, many did not We also planted three Rutgers dogwoods—two lived one did not. Hundreds of spring bulbs were installed along the drive that first autumn—some have persisted, many have not—the triumphs and pitfalls of gardening.

Fuller Drive has a strong cadence of landscape drama. You enter through the stone pillars immediately passing the detention pond on your right and low moist woodland to your left. After going past the gatehouse, the drive begins to rise, introducing you to a mixed woodland of hardwoods and white and pitch pine. The road levels and you pass a field on your right and more forest rising to the left. As the drive rises again you make your way through the Harrington Orchard. The drive levels and you find yourself at the parking lots and a straight road that leads to a drop-off area for the Education and Visitors Center.

Multitasking being the rule, we were in the thick of designing the Education and Visitors Center, the adjacent Entry Court, and fund raising for what we called Phase II. We worked primarily with Earl Pope, principal architect, and Kevin Chroback, associate architect. Kevin was the go to guy onsite when supervision was required. The footprint of the building was established during the master planning process, a long linear structure, two stories with a mezzanine on the west, and one story with a mezzanine on the east. This would accommodate the natural slope of the field as the old barn had for two hundred years.

The layout for the building was fairly simple: three classrooms on the main level, one designed as a theater and two connected by a folding door which would convert to a larger space to accommodate 150 people. A gift shop and a large exhibition space were also planned for the main level along with a small service pantry connecting to a kitchen on the lower level. The library and kitchen would be on the lower level along with a fourth classroom for cooking demonstrations and children's activities. Restrooms would exist on all three floors, the larger on the main visitors' level with coat racks. There would be plenty of storage on all floors, a receptionist's window, drinking fountains and the all-important pay phone. We made sure there was enough wiring and conduits to support an automated phone system and any future technology needs as reliance on computers was growing daily. We tried to anticipate every possible requirement we might have. Last but not least, was a large gathering space on the main floor with a high ceiling that could accommodate the Hadwen Victorian tall clock.

Artist's rendering of the Stoddard Education and Visitors Center, 1989

From the Inside Out

The old barn in the process of deconstruction, 1992

The old Barn

The circa-1800 barn and the 1920s dairy barn had to be removed. After an article appeared in the *Worcester Telegram and Gazette* we received several calls regarding the old five-bay barn. One person was interested in the barn for two separate projects, one in Hingham the other on Martha's Vineyard. He agreed to pay us five thousand dollars to remove the barn and clean up the site.

The Inferno

As we dealt with the historic barn, we also had to address the dairy wing. This was a challenge because the roof was constructed with asbestos shingles. At no small expense, the shingles had to be carefully removed one by one, put in heavy plastic bags, then into a dumpster to be transported off the property. The remainder of the wing was demolished and piled high on one of the open fields. One calm and snowy Sunday I got it into my head to set a match to the pile. I never saw anything burn as fast. At the height of the blaze, I watched paralyzed with fear that it might get out of control. As quickly as it flared, it subsided and was burned out within a couple of hours—lucky me.

You can't break ground until you have a building permit from the town building inspector. Even though we and the inspector had periodically met with the architects during the design process, he pronounced that the building was three feet higher than the building code allowed. He was referencing the portion of the west façade that included the library windows, general west side egress, and entrance to the lower classroom. The remainder of the west side was compliant with the local building code. We felt that this decision by the inspector was unreasonable. We could have requested a variance but this would have delayed construction by a year. In the end, the architects redesigned the west side in a way that would still give us access from the outside but satisfied the town. A one step retaining wall satisfied the code. To accomplish this a staircase was added for access to the lower level—awkward but doable.

With this major hiccup resolved, we scheduled the ground breaking for Thursday, September 24, 1992. Trustees and donors were present as Helen Stoddard broke ground with the turn of a shovel. Helen had pledged $1.5 million to the project. The Stoddard Education and Visitors Center cost $2.8 million to build.

Our Pet Rock

Fifty or so feet off the driveway and fifty feet from the west side of the old barn, was a large boulder. It was apparently a stone too large to move for the generation of farmers who tilled the soil since the 1720s. We loved this rock from the moment we saw Tower Hill Farm in 1984. Two Adirondack chairs were placed next to it for people to sit and enjoy the view of Mt. Wachusett. The boulder seemed to draw children like a magnet. Alison Kenary was a frequent visitor in those early days. Pregnant with her fifth child and with her four children in tow, Allison

From the Inside Out

Our pet rock, 1989

often enjoyed a respite in one of those Adirondack chairs as the kids clambered on the rock. Time passes quickly. One of her sons, Jim, is now my financial advisor.

The boulder, however, stood in the way of construction and had to be removed. I was not keen on this scenario. It had been located on the site plan for the education building and had appeared to fall safely in the northeast border of the Entry Court. Joann and I measured the distance of the rock from the northwest corner of the Farmhouse and the northern most granite post of the Farmhouse curb. By doing this, the boulder could be placed back in its original location—another Watteau moment for Joann and me. All this planning came to fruition and today the rock rests quietly under the shade of a weeping Katsura tree.

Stoddard Education and Visitors Center under construction, 1989

This same Katsura was a gift from the O'Connell family in memory of Lawrence O'Connell. During the ceremonial planting the family placed a SPAG's tote bag filled with letters and drawings in the hole. Now adults, the children had sent or given them to their father when they were young.

Construction went quickly and without incident. When the decision came to determine a choice of roofing material, trustee Anita Hooker spoke up and said that real, as opposed to fake, slate *must* be used. Everyone agreed. Anita also insisted on a warm brown color of stain for the siding. A compatible green color was used for the trim.

I led the charge concerning changing the paint color of the Farmhouse—from the stark white it had been for decades to a warmer color to go along with the Education and Visitors Center. The goal was to "not have the Farmhouse stick out like a sore thumb." Most everyone agreed. Anita and I and a few other color-minded people drove around looking at paint colors on similar old houses. We chose a color called "dune." It looked great.

Fourth edition of the Marshall-Rausch 50-year plan for Tower Hill. After each phase was completed, the plan was updated to show the finished areas in detail. This 2011 edition shows Tower Hill at the completion of Phase IVA.

The Farmhouse, c. 2011, situated above grade from the Jeppson Terrace. To the right is the Japanese umbrella pine, gift of Robert Bunting in memory of his wife Dorothy.

From the Collections of Tower Hill Botanic Garden, Boylston, MA

The beautiful roundel with *Magnolia x loebneri* 'Merrill' in the Jacqueline Harley Harrington Cottage Garden due east of the Farmhouse. The tree is on axis with the shed door.

Courtesy of Robert Zeleniak, 2011

The Nathaniel Thayer Dexter Lawn Garden south of the Cottage Garden, terminating on the twin pergolas.
Courtesy of Robert Zeleniak, 2006

The twin pergolas looking northeast from the Edith J. Beals Secret Garden, c. 1994.
From the Collections of Tower Hill Botanic Garden, Boylston, MA

Frank L. Harrington, Sr., Orchard with the Stearns Lothrop
Davenport collection of pre-20th-century apples, c. 2010
Courtesy of John Trexler

The million-dollar view looking northwest towards Mt. Wachusett
from the summit of Tower Hill.
From the Collections of Tower Hill Botanic Garden, Boylston, MA

Stoddard Education and Visitors Center with 2010 addition of the Morgan Reception Gateway. The original pedimented section (left) was completed in 1994 through the generous support of the Stoddard Charitable Trust and Mrs. Robert (Helen) W. Stoddard.

Views of the E. Stanley and Alice M. Wright Entry Garden with the beautiful entry pavilion, part of Phase III.

Photos courtesy of Robert Zeleniak, 2011

The Orangerie at dusk, summer 2004. The Orangerie was dedicated in 1999, a gift of Julia Agrippina.
Courtesy of Robert Nash Studios, 2004

Interior view of the Orangerie, winter 2010
Courtesy of Robert Zeleniak, 2010

East axis, Orangerie
Courtesy of Robert Zeleniak, 2004

The Kinship Arbor in the Systematic Garden is constructed of 16 cast-iron columns salvaged from a razed building in Boston. The arbor was a gift of Barbara Allen Booth and part of Capital Campaign III. It was designed by Blair Hines.
Courtesy of Robert Zeleniak, 2011

Above: Long south to north axis from north side of Orangerie to Victorian Fountain and Kinship Arbor

Right: Monocot pool in its summer glory

Left: The mist fountain of the Daniel Farber Primordial Pool, looking north to the Kinship Arbor

Photos courtesy of Robert Zeleniak, 2013

The Robert Jay Folly, gift of Tay Ann Jay. The Folly is known as the Temple of Apollo and the Muses. Insert: Ciborowski Cupid, the only anatomically correct statue at Tower Hill.

From the Collections of Tower Hill Botanic Garden, Boylston, MA

Inset of Cupid courtesy of Robert Zeleniak, 2012

Looking east towards the Hope Hartwell Spear Wildlife Pond, gift of her husband Ivan. The George F. and Sybil H. Fuller Rustic Pavilion is to the left.

Bronze heron statues (named after John and Frannie Herron), gift of Robert Booth, in the Wildlife Garden.

Photos courtesy of Robert Zeleniak, 2011

The Moss Steps, gift of Valerie Loring and Judith King in memory of their mother Helen E. Stoddard. They represent an interpretation of the original steps from the Stoddard Garden designed by Fletcher Steele. They were designed and engineered by Blair Hines and sited by John Trexler, 2002.

Pliny's Fountain, gift of Shirley and Peter Williams in memory of Henry Horner, conceived by John Trexler, designed by Blair Hines, 2000.

Photos courtesy of Robert Zeleniak, 2011

Clockwise from top: Limonaia interior soon after it was open in 2010, gift of the George F. and Sybil H. Fuller Foundation and Marillyn Zacharis; John on his mother's honorary bench in the Limonaia; the Wilson Lemon.

Photos courtesy of Robert Zeleniak, 2010, 2011

Above: Domitian's Pool, gift of Kitty Ferguson, fashioned after an atrium pool in Domus Augustana, Palatine Hill, Rome. Kitty loved the outline.

Above: Pollux one of the two bronze turtle fountains commanding Domitian's Pool, gift of Chloe Nester Sundberg, sculpted by Priscilla Deichmann.

Left: Greenhouse horticulturist Christian Primeau's summer container display in the northwest corner of Winter Garden.

Above: The Rose Ellipse, conceived by John Trexler as a place holder for the east side of the Visitors Center, Phase IVB.

Below: In the foreground, Pollux shooting water at his twin Castor. The north wall of the Limonaia is in the background.

Photos on spread courtesy of Robert Zeleniak, 2012, 2014

Latin for "Make Haste Slowly," *Festina Lente* is attributed to Augustus Caesar, 63 B.C.-14 A.D., Roman emperor, who adopted the phrase as his motto. It was a favorite quote of Tower Hill's dear friend and benefactor Julia Agrippina a.k.a. Louise Doyle. The words are mounted in her honor on the south façade of the Limonaia.

From the Collections of Tower Hill Botanic Garden, Boylston, MA

The dedication party for the Stoddard Center was quite an affair with speeches, music, and a delicious banquet. The guest of honor that evening was Helen Stoddard. She was dressed in a stunning black gown with a lace top. As Ginger Este serenaded the crowd from the balcony overlooking the Great Hall singing G.F. Handel's "Verdant Meadows," Mrs. Stoddard stood directly beneath the candled chandelier. Mid-way through the performance one of the candles flared, creating a stalactite of wax that grew in size by the second until it broke off from its own weight. I was standing against the south wall and watched in horror as this disaster unfolded. The hot wax fell onto Mrs. Stoddard's left lace-covered shoulder. Others were oblivious to the incident. As the group made its way to dinner in the large classroom, I approached Mrs. Stoddard to see if she was all right. She smiled and said, "You're paying for the dry cleaning." Relieved, I took her arm as we walked in to dinner. Helen, Dick Dearborn, President of WCHS, architect Earl Pope and I each gave speeches.

Helen always described our fundraising results as "Manna from heaven." Within the museum world we were getting a reputation for raising large amounts of money in record time.

Helen Stoddard had a favorite poem she would often quote. She requested that a portion of the poem be on the bronze dedication plaque to be mounted in the south vestibule. The entire poem is as follows:

MY GARDEN
Thomas Edward Brown 1830-1897

A GARDEN is a lovesome thing, God wot!
Rose plot,
Fringed pool,
Ferned grot-
The veriest school
Of peace; and yet the fool
Contends that God is not-
Not God! In gardens! when the eve is cool?
Nay, but I have a sign;
Tis very sure God walks in mine.

Guests enjoy drinks and hors d'oeuvre under the candled chandelier in the Great Hall at the Stoddard Education and Visitors Center gala, 1994

Helen Stoddard at the podium during the gala

From the Inside Out

Cleopatra

Helen was a formidable and imperious individual, two traits that made her interesting and forthright. Much of her energy went into making and maintaining her beloved garden and supporting the many cultural institutions in Worcester. In the fourteen years I knew her, we spent a lot of time together. One winter's eve after work, I stopped by her home for a cocktail. Helen was becoming impatient with her cook who was having difficulty discerning a cocktail glass from a wine glass. Helen's stern reprimand made the woman cry and leave the room. I boldly scolded Helen for being overly harsh and asked who she had been in former life. Without hesitation, she proclaimed she was the queen of Egypt and had cut off lots of heads. This made us both laugh. We settled down with our drinks and had a lively conversation.

—ɷ—

Another angel subtly began to bestow her largess, Mrs. Howard Booth—Barbara Allen Booth—took an interest in the proposed Oak Allée to the north of the north vestibule of the Stoddard Education and Visitors Center. She made an appointment to discuss the trees that were to be planted.

I had divided the allée into ten pairs of oak trees. I called them "couple trees." There would be five species represented, all but one indigenous to Massachusetts. Barbara and I sat in the large parlor of the Farmhouse in chairs that had been made for the library on Elm Street. I gave her a full report on the landscape importance of the allée and how it would be used as a teaching tool for oak trees, allées, and windbreaks. Prepared right then and there to contribute $25,000 for a pair of trees, she handed me a check and politely exited. A week later she called and asked if she could come and see me. We sat in the same two chairs and she announced that she would like to buy another pair of trees. I asked if she was sure.

"John," she said, "When the cookies are passed, take one."

The following week we repeated the same scenario. On week four

Barbara Booth planting the first oak of Pliny's Allée, 1993

she called and asked to meet once again. This time she purchased the remaining trees, a total of $250,000. Talk about cookies!

The acquisition of all ten pairs of trees gave Barbara Booth the naming rights to the allée. She chose to name the allée in memory of her brother, George Pliny Allen, who had died in WWII in an airplane crash over the Ploesti Oil Fields in Romania. The allée was affectionately named Pliny's Allée.

From the Inside Out

Pliny's Allée, 2003

The allée was planted in 1993 just as the Stoddard Center was completed. Barbara had one request. She wanted to bury a coin under the first tree planted. Her brother Pliny had the habit of burying his allowance in a box at the base of a tree at Allen Acres, the family's country estate in Spencer. Her father gave silver dollars as allowance. A silver dollar was placed in the hole of an English Oak, the one non-native species. Why English oak? Because it is a tree species in the cemetery where Pliny is buried in Belgium. The silver dollar chosen had the profile of Dwight D. Eisenhower. I suggested we also include a Roman coin with the profile of the emperor Trajan, a Roman silver denarius. The reason for these two coins: Eisenhower was commander of the allied forces in Europe while Pliny served; Trajan was the commander in chief of the Roman military for whom Pliny the Younger served in the early second century. Barbara agreed that telling the story of the two Plinys of the first and second millennia would give a richer interpretation to the public. The Eisenhower coin was a gift from Barbara; the Trajan coin was a gift from me (by coincidence I had bought one in London a year earlier). The coins were put in a plastic case and placed in the hole. Barbara put in the first shovel of soil.

On the occasion of Barbara's 90th birthday, her children, Pene, Brenda and Geof, supported the planting of the twin shrub border along the length of Pliny's Allée. They were named the Autumn Borders for the beautiful fall color of the oakleaf hydrangea (*Hydrangea quercifolia*), Virginia sweetspire (*Itea virginica*), large fothergilla (*Fothergilla major*), and witch hazel, (*Hamamelis virginiana*). We also planted a species of crocus (*Crocus thomasinianus*) for early spring bloom.

A Tray of Cookies

Barbara loved Tower Hill and she and I developed a close relationship. Her list of gifts to the Horticultural Society over a span of fifteen years are as follows: the flag pole and mill stone (in memory of her father), twin statues of the god Janus made by artist Tom O'Connell at the south end of the allée to commemorate the turn of the twenty-first century, the Friendship Urn in the Inner Park, the twin lead *putti* in the Systematic Garden, the Kinship Arbor in the Systematic Garden, the lead statues of the Four Seasons with their pedestals in the Secret Garden. She also funded the complete replacement of windows for the Farmhouse and a video projector for the theater. She was pragmatic and wanted to see the results of her largess—a great friend.

A little more about the "herms" of Janus. True to the classical tradition, Barbara liked the idea of flanking the allée with sculpture, and because of the commemoration of the beginning of the third millennium CE, thought herms of the Roman god Janus would be appropriate. Janus is the two-faced god. One is the face of youth looking to the east or the beginning of the day and the other is the face of age looking to the west to the day's end. A herm is just the head and shoulders of the subject sitting on a tapered pedestal with the male genitalia sculpted in the correct location. In order not to offend the sensibilities of the garden visitor, this detail is represented by the letter "T." The letter is upside-down for the face of youth—truly subliminal.

From the Inside Out

The "birdhouse for people" in the Wildlife Garden, 1995

WILDLIFE GARDEN

An area dear to my heart was always the Wildlife Garden, comprising approximately five acres on the Master Plan. It possessed a variety of habitats—wet, dry, and rocky. The sections were framed by intersecting paths, one being the Loop Trail. The first section contained a vernal pool which had been used as a dump by the various owners of the farm for at least two hundred years. We began the clean-up effort as early as 1987. We wanted to highlight the vernal pool and the flora that framed it. Invasive plants aggressively impaired the native plants. With the help of the Trail Blazers, a group of stalwart volunteers that dedicated weekend time to the effort, we systematically declared war on the invasives—bittersweet, shrub honeysuckle and buckthorn. It was a long conflict with well-focused battles. The Worcester Garden Club was so impressed that they pledged five thousand dollars toward the building of a structure that would act as a viewing house for watching birds. Anita Hooker's daughter, Nan Norseen, designed and constructed the garden house modeled on one she had built at her mother's property, Misty Meadows, in Bolton. Our only instructions were that it look like a "birdhouse for people." The Trailblazers and I continued to fuss with the Wildlife Garden until I retired from Tower Hill in early 2012.

Magnolia Tree

In late April 1984, I gave a tree walk at Elm Park, one of the public parks in Worcester. I risked my life and the life of the one person who had joined me to cross busy Park Avenue to look at the trees adjacent to the Rogers-Kennedy Memorial. I had been led to believe the Olmstead Brothers designed the planting in the 1930s. Two trees stood out, a Carolina silverbell (*Halesia carolina*) and a magnolia (*Magnolia tripetala*). Having moved to the west side of Worcester in October of 1984, I drove past these trees on a regular basis.

Hurricane Gloria battered Massachusetts in September of 1985 and toppled many trees in Worcester. One of the trees was the magnolia. After the storm passed Bob and I took a drive to assess the damage. We pulled over to the side of the road and inspected the fallen hulk of the magnolia. There were dozens of "fruiting cones" on the ground and the propagator in me readily picked up as many as possible. That night I extracted at least a hundred seeds and sowed them in a large plastic flat the next day. The following spring, one seed out of a hundred germinated. Once the seedling had one set of true leaves, I potted it in a six-inch pot. I continued to nurture it for six years. In spring of 1993, I planted the tree just to the southwest of the "birdhouse for people." The hope was that the tree would eventually begin to seed in the Wildlife Garden, just as it had in the moist woods at Skylands. A seedling did appear. It was six feet tall in 2015.

CHAPTER SIX

A Garden of People

No sooner was the Stoddard Education and Visitors Center opened and the Pliny's Alleé planted that we began brainstorming Phase III. At its conclusion, we dedicated the Orangerie, Entry Garden, parking lots, Systematic Garden, Pliny's Fountain, Inner Park, Wildlife Pond, flag pole and Moss Steps. Whew!

In June of 1995, the Society received a gift of one million dollars—*manna from heaven*. The donor was insistent that she remain anonymous but I was required to give her name to the board of trustees. It was, in fact, Louise Doyle, the quiet lady from Leominster, who had attended the joint meeting with the Trustees of Reservations regarding our purchase of Tower Hill Farm in 1985. She had been keeping an eye on the Worcester County Horticultural Society and was impressed with the progress we had made over the last ten years. Louise's donation pushed Phase III into high gear and so impressed the Worcester and Boston foundations that they raised their gifts from their Phase II levels. Louise had been consistently making year-end donations to the tune of $50,000 to $100,000. Our Phase III campaign goal was $7.5 million.

Above: Black gum (*Nyssa sylvatica*)

Louise joined me in my passion for Roman history. On one visit she asked if I knew about Julia Agrippina.

"Which one? Agrippina the elder or younger."

"The younger," she said and I responded in the affirmative.

Her next question was, "Who was her husband?"

"First or second husband?" I asked.

"First."

"I don't know," I answered.

"Gnaeus Ahenobarbus," she said, delighted to show off her superior knowledge.

It became clear that Louise had a thing for Julia Agrippina the younger. Agrippina was the great granddaughter of Caesar Augustus and Mark Antony, granddaughter of Marcus Agrippa and Julia the elder, daughter of Germanicus, sister to Emperor Caligula, third wife to the Emperor Claudius (also her uncle), and mother to the emperor Nero (who eventually had her murdered). Louise asked me to call her "Grip." She in turn called me "Gus" because she thought I was the personification of Augustus (which appealed immensely to my vanity). To maintain a level of anonymity, she preferred her gifts to Tower Hill be acknowledged as from "Julia Agrippina."

Gus and Grip, c. 2005

My Travels

John on a trip to Egypt in 2010

I was fortunate to travel the world during my tenure as director, both personally and on tours sponsored by WCHS. Our first trip with the Society was a tour of Germany and Austria in 1985, specifically the cities and environs of Munich, Salzburg, and Vienna. The primary objectives were to see gardens, castles and palaces. In Munich we toured the Residenz, Munich Botanic Garden and Nymphenburg Palace and gardens. In the environs we saw the royal residences of Neuschwanstein, Hohenschwangau, Linderhof and Herrenchiemsee. We visited Mirabell Palace and gardens in Salzburg, and also the extraordinary Italianate Hellbrunn palace and gardens, the most elaborate water gardens outside Italy. In Vienna we perused Schönbrunn, the Belvedere Palace and gardens and the Vienna Botanic Garden.

In 1988, a group travelled to Leningrad (St. Petersburg) as part of the "sister cities" collaborative, a program sponsored by Sister Cities International (SCI), a nonprofit citizen diplomacy network that creates partnerships between communities in the United States and those in other countries. Perhaps due to my odd *karma*, we arrived in Russia and there was no one to welcome us. As it turned out, the Russians had no idea we were coming—talk about a disconnection. The visit was hastily organized by the next morning and the Russians turned out to be the best of hosts. The city of Leningrad was designed to be at its most beautiful in the winter and our hosts showed us the Winter Garden, Pavlovsk Park and garden, Piskaryovskoye Memorial Cemetery, the Catherine Palace and garden and the Hermitage.

After my traveling companions returned to Worcester, I took a side trip to Frankfurt to see the new state-of-the-art greenhouses at the Frankfurt Botanic Garden. Much had been written about them and I wanted to find out if they were worth emulating at Tower Hill. They were not. The day I was to fly home, I received word from Bob that my father had died. It was a difficult homecoming.

Organized perfectly by Debi Hogan, our Education Coordinator, the next WCHS-sponsored trip was to England in 1993. We began in the Cotswolds, the highlight being the garden of Rosemary Verey and the town of Cirencester. From there we travelled to London to tour the Royal Botanic Garden at Kew and the Royal Horticultural Society Gardens at Wisley. We were also fortunate to experience the Chelsea Flower Show and the Physic Gardens. We visited Sezincote, a two hundred-year-old house designed as a Mogul Indian palace and set in a romantic landscape of temples, grottoes, waterfalls and canals reminiscent of the Taj Mahal. We also saw Sissinghurst, Blenheim Palace and gardens, and Stourhead.

In 1995, I participated in a co-sponsored, ten-day trip to China. We started in Shanghai where we saw the magnificent zen garden, then a train ride to Suzhou where we visited three gardens. At the zen garden at Lake Tai, I collected seeds of Chinese wingnut (*Pterocarya stenoptera*). We grew this tree successfully for a few years at Tower Hill until it succumbed to a particularly cold winter.

Three days were spent on the Yangtze River and the three gorges, the most scenic section of the river and the location of the Three Gorges

A Garden of People

Dam. We flew to Xi'an to see the Terracotta Army of Qin Shi Huang, the first Emperor of China. The trip concluded in Beijing and environs with visits to the Great Wall, the Forbidden City, and the beautiful Summer Palace and garden.

Thanks to WCHS trustee and friend Jeremy O'Connell and his organizational skills, he and I went to Rome, Naples, and Pompeii in 2001. This initiated an obsessive need to visit Rome twice a year for ten years. I continue my visits but not quite as obsessively.

My personal travels have also taken me to Lombardy, Veneto, Tuscany, Latium, Campania, Apulia, and Sicily regions of Italy. I have wallowed in the history and pleasures of Morocco, Egypt, Croatia, Montenegro, Slovenia and Costa Rica.

A Lesson in Astronomy

In October 1987, Bob and I sold our house in Worcester and bought 16 School Street in Boylston with only a half-mile commute to Tower Hill. Our first Christmas tree was a balled and burlapped white fir

The backyard patio at 16 School Street, Boylston. Over the course of twenty-seven years, John and Bob developed the landscape into a series of display gardens.

(*Abies concolor*). I pre-dug a hole to receive it on December 26 after its decorated stint indoors. The tree was sited on the southeast corner of our property and grew fast and tall. Ten or so years later, I received a call from the reclusive neighbor on our southern boundary. She was worried that the tree was going to cast shade on her house. I was quick to explain that it was located to the north of her house and she need not be concerned.

"What's your point?" she asked.

"My point? My point is, the sun rises in the east, sets in the west and casts shadows from south to north." In spite of my assurances, she remained confused.

Belvedere

That same year, trustee Ken Hedenburg came to me to discuss the building of a memorial for his wife Janette. Because she had loved music, he thought that perhaps a bandstand might be appropriate. There was no bandstand specified on the Master Plan other than the amphitheater and that came at an enormous cost. On the plan I pointed out where there were to be several viewing pavilions located. The one that most appealed to Ken was the proposed "Belvedere" overlooking the reservoir and Mt. Wachusett.

We walked out to the leaching field (much prettier than it sounds) at the base of the path to the Tower Hill summit to look over the area where the Belvedere would be situated. The exact location had not yet been cleared, but since it was early spring and there were no leaves on the trees, he was able get an impression of the spectacular view. That night I executed a scale drawing of a rectilinear structure with eight Tuscan columns and sent it to Ken. He liked the design very much but of course wanted to know the cost. From experience I knew that we would have to double the actual construction cost in order to endow the continuing maintenance expenses. He tentatively agreed to the number and I showed the drawings to our local Bow House representative. The quote was $13,000 installed. Ken pledged $30,000. His one concern

The Hedenburg Belvedere with views of Mt. Wachusett and the reservoir

was—could the view be preserved since some trees would need to be routinely cut or pruned on property that did not belong to the Society. The neighbors agreed, in writing, to give us access going forward. The Belvedere was dedicated in October 1995 with seventy-five of Ken and Janette's friends attending.

Belvedere Bonus

The Belvedere is one of the most popular destinations at Tower Hill. One spring day a few years after the dedication, I crossed paths with a young woman and her infant son. I chatted her up a bit and asked her how she was enjoying her visit.

"It's a wonderful place," she said, "I'm on my way to the Belvedere. Today is my son's first birthday."

"Enjoy the Belvedere," was my parting comment.

"I will. It's where my son was conceived."

Too much information!

Entry Garden and Entry Court

Since its unveiling in 1988, the Master Plan had displayed a schematic design of the Entry Garden. We chose Halverson Company to flesh out the details of the design. Blair Hines, a member of the Halverson team, was the lead landscape architect on the project. The general idea was that the garden be a "sampler" of the plant collection themes at Tower Hill—ornamental, economic and ecologic—and also a garden to inspire homeowners with interesting combinations of readily accessible plants. The ornamental plants were selected from lists in two books, one on trees, *Plants That Merit Attention: Trees* and the other on shrubs, *Plants That Merit Attention: Shrubs*, published by the Garden Club of America in 1986 and 1996 respectively.

Blair designed an octagonal pavilion as the gateway for the garden. Four sides of the octagon were open portals, two aiming the visitor to the Stoddard Center and the other two leading the visitor either to the Lawn Garden or to an inner path of the Entry Garden. The material was rough sawn oak—mortise and tenon construction—reminiscent of the Farmhouse and old barn. Using the well-known design process called "trial and error," I designed an octagonal copper lantern for the peak of the pavilion. The entire structure was built in Vermont and assembled at Tower Hill.

The opening of the Entry Garden and the groundbreaking for the Orangerie were held together on October 19, 1997.

A fountain in the form of an obelisk was added to the landscape in August 2000. It was a gift from John and Marianne Jeppson in honor of their daughter Ingrid, who was a past trustee of WCHS. The obelisk, designed and executed by Tom O'Connell, is a wildly intricate concrete cast—a treasure to be sure.

A smaller section of the Entry Garden was the so-called Entry Court. It was located on the east side of the driveway and built during the construction of the Stoddard Education and Visitors Center. When the west side of the driveway portion was added during Phase III, we had two donors vying for the naming rights to the entire garden. One donor

Construction of the Entry Pavilion and Garden, 1997

pledged $200,000 and the other $150,000. It was a difficult problem but a good one to have. Like the biblical King Solomon, I split the garden in two, giving the west side to the first donor and the east side to the latter. The Entry Garden was named in honor of E. Stanley and Alice M. Wright and the Entry Court in memory of W. Robert Mill and Thomas Smith. Both donor groups were satisfied.

Moral of story—stay flexible, and don't let them see you sweat.

Orangerie

We interviewed three architects and three landscape architects to design Phase III in July 1995. Homsey Architects from Wilmington, Delaware, were selected to design the Orangerie and, as mentioned, Halvorson Design from Boston did the design and site work for the Entry Garden.

The Napkin

Soon after the contract with Homesy was signed, Lenny Sophrin, the lead architect on the two-man team, came to meet with the Building Committee. When the day long meeting was concluded, he came back to our home at 16 School Street to find out more about my personal vision for the Orangerie over drinks. I described two buildings I thought should be used as models: the display greenhouse at the Biltmore estate in Ashville, North Carolina, and a building illustrated in *Miller's Dictionary of Gardening*, an early nineteenth-century book in the Tower Hill library. Lenny immediately started sketching on a cocktail napkin.

"Is this what you're thinking?" he asked.

"Yes."

Four years later the completed Orangerie was a more detailed version of that exact sketch on the napkin.

Napkins aside, the real design process was long and at times arduous. Some members of the Orangerie Committee had difficulty articulating their visions for the building. Lenny and his assistant Curtis Harkin bent over backwards trying to intrepret their ideas. The long and short of it—form follows function. The function of the building was to be an ornamental greenhouse where plants could be successfully grown in the cold season and then be moved outside for display in the growing season. This would allow the building to be used for social events, such as weddings, during the warmer growing season. The schematic drawings were approved and the construction drawing phase began in 1996. Louise Doyle, a.k.a. Julia Agrippina, the major donor to the project, was pleased at the progress of design.

Keeping in mind the two proposed adjoining gardens—the Winter Garden south of the Orangerie and the Systematic Garden to the north—Blair Hines did a remarkable job melding the rough grades. He also took the lead in the finish work on the parking lots and Entry Garden. We kept one eye on the Orangerie, the other on the Entry

Sid Callahan, c. 2004

Garden as we raised capital and operating revenue.

The Phase I goal of $2.5 million had been raised with the help of Newtel Associates. Callahan-McIntyre from Worcester assisted us in reaching our goal of $5.5 million for Phase II. $7.5 million was raised in house with our skilled development staff for Phase III. Phase II and III totals both included successful challenge grants from the Kresge Foundation headquartered in Troy, Michigan.

—⁂—

Sid Callahan was president of WCHS during the "Orangerie years" (1995-1999). She and I were a good team. Sid was well-connected to the Worcester community and her husband Frank was extraordinarily handy. He undertook projects that helped set a decorative standard inside and outside the buildings. When it came to raising money, Sid had a very succinct mantra, "You're only as good as your last check." (she gives credit to her friend Tay Ann Jay for this quote). It was duly acknowledged and appreciated that you had supported Phase I and/or II, but how will you support Phase III?

The Orangerie under construction, 1998

*One of a pair of wall fountainheads in the Orangerie
donated by Nancy Grimes in memory of her husband Humphrey Sutton*

This is not as crass as it sounds—just a reality in the world of nonprofits. The years she was president were some of the most fulfilling of my career.

The details of the Orangerie design were masterful. Lenny and Curtis developed a cadence of ceiling heights. They started with the low Milton Gallery, then went to a higher vestibule between classrooms A and B, which then led into the Fern Gallery that embraces the Orangerie on the west, north and east sides, and finally to the Orangerie itself which has a ceiling height of thirty feet at its apex.

The building is supported by Roman, or rounded, arches and Jack, or flat, arches which are both decorative and load bearing. The width of the wall that separates the Orangerie from the Fern Gallery accommodates the heating system and provides utility closets. I can take credit for designing the south-facing folding doors which I presented to the architects using a scale model. We wanted to install two water features on the north and south facing walls. Nancy Grimes of New England Garden Ornaments suggested lead cisterns with a Leaf-Man and Leaf-Woman as fountainheads. She presented them as her gift to Phase III in memory of her husband Humphrey Sutton.

The Wilson Lemon

Earnest H. Wilson (1876–1930) was an extraordinarily successful plant explorer. His first three expeditions to China were sponsored by the English nursery, James Veitch and Sons. On his third expedition, he was caught in an avalanche resulting in a broken leg. During his convalescence, he benefited from the healthy juice of lemons and noticed that the locals grew them easily in their homes. During his days as Associate Director of the Arnold Arboretum in Jamaica Plains, Massachusetts, he cultured a lemon tree from seeds he had brought back and grew it in his office. Ben Blackburn, who I worked with at the Willowwood Arboretum in New Jersey, shared this story with me. Wilson had given him a cutting of his lemon plant while Ben was an Arboretum intern and he rooted and cultured it in turn at Willowwood.

Ben passed along a cutting to Tom Buchter, my friend and mentor, who grew it at Skylands. Tom then gave a rooted cutting to me and I eventually shared it with Tower Hill to be cultured in the Orangerie and later in the Limonaia. I now have a plant at my home in Westborough, Massachusetts. And so on—this is how plants are propagated and passed on.

As a tragic postscript, Wilson and his wife died in an automobile accident in Worcester after giving a lecture at 30 Elm Street.

The First Gift

As the Stoddard Center neared completion, Nancy and Humphrey presented Tower Hill with a reproduction of the "Pope Urn." The original Pope Urn was designed for Alexander Pope by William Kent to adorn his eighteenth-century estate, Twickenham, on the Thames River in England. I decided it would be most effective if it was displayed in a natural setting. The chosen location was the visual terminus of Pliny's Path directly off the Loop Trail in an area that was later to become the

Left: *the Pope Urn in the Inner Park, 1999*
Right: *Nancy Grimes installs the Friendship Urn, given by Barbara Booth*

A Garden of People

Inner Park or native plant garden. Pliny's Path connects the terminus (Pliny's Fountain) of the allée with the Inner Park and the Belvedere.

The Pope Urn inspired other donors and the decorative theme in the Park became eighteenth-century English naturalistic. Added over a period of fifteen years were other garden ornaments and structures: the Friendship Urn donated by Barbara Booth, the Folly from Tay Ann Jay, the statues of Eros and Diana from Henry Ciborowski, and the Temple of Peace from Arthur and Martha Pappas.

Nancy and Humphrey made another gift, a "term"—in statuary, meaning a human head and torso that continues as a square tapering pillar—of the god Pan, which became the centerpiece of the Clearing on the Loop Trail. It was expertly situated by Joann Vieira.

—m—

Due to the monumental nature of the iron arches that supported the roof structure of the Orangerie, construction of the building was dramatic. More than any other project the Orangerie caught the imagination of visitors.

As we were juggling the daily demands of the complex building project, we were also considering the plants to be displayed. Joann, John Mapel, Greenhouse Horticulturist, and I made list of plants suited to a cool greenhouse—forty-five to fifty degrees at night. John and I travelled to southern Florida and visited all the major nurseries that would ship plants north. The trip was a success and the plants were slated to ship in late summer of 1998. The schedule was determined by the promised completion date of the contractor. As we say, the best-laid plans don't always fall together. The building was delayed and the plants, despite our best efforts, got frosted. Eighty percent of them survived but sadly we lost all the palms. The good news was that they were comparatively inexpensive and we replaced them the following spring. They looked perfect for the dedication.

Louise Doyle was the guest of honor at the dedication of the Orangerie. Being Louise, she wanted spaces in the adjoining Stoddard Center to look a "certain way." Many weeks, and a hundred thousand dollars later, the main floor got a makeover. White walls became a subdued beige; the brick fireplace was veneered in stone; the chandelier was nickel-plated and the doors of the Great Hall received Roman shades. Wood blinds and heavy green curtains were installed in classrooms A and B. It was hard to say no to Louise considering her generosity but the process strained everyone's nerves. It was the one and only time I felt hostage to a donor. The results were applauded by the general public and that's all that mattered. And, of course, Louise was happy.

In spite of her aversion to public speaking, Louise gave the following speech at the dedication of the Orangerie on January 29, 1999:

> One bright day in 1984, Dame Fortune and the celestial angels smiled on the Worcester County Horticultural Society when John Trexler appeared on the horizon. Tonight, we and the trees and the flowers and the plants and the grass under the snow and the squirrels in their dens—we are all here to sing his praises and to thank him and show our heartfelt appreciation and sincere admiration. He had vision, the inspiration and the will to make this wonderful Orangerie happen.
>
> John loves everything Roman and particularly admires Caesar Augustus, Imperator Maximus, who gave Rome a heart and a soul; so indeed did John give Tower Hill a heart and a soul, building—structurally and aesthetically magnificent—another Eden, a demi-paradise, a precious place set in the rolling hills of Central Massachusetts.
>
> It is my happy privilege and tremendous pleasure to name it the "Orangerie." It is truly an oasis, a haven from the rush of modern life, a place of refuge and tranquility, and, as it will say in Latin on the cornice "Si Caelum In Terra Sit Haec Id Est Latitia Aeterna"— If there is heaven on earth, this is it, joy everlasting!

I was truly honored by Louise's words but in my response I outlined that the Orangerie was the result of the vision and spirit of many:

> The idea of incorporating a display greenhouse in the style of an eighteenth century Orangerie as part of the Horticultural Society's planned garden was first discussed in January 1984. We stand here

A Garden of People

together on this lovely January evening fifteen years later, dedicating this magnificent 14,000 square-foot Orangerie addition to the Stoddard Education and Visitors Center. The exhaustive progress the Society has made over the years is due to two primary reasons. First, the faithful and unwavering respect for the Tower Hill Master Plan, and second, the faithful and unwavering support of the membership and community. All of you gathered here this evening have played a significant role in financing, planning, designing, building, and caring for the this magnificent structure. As the late Helen Stoddard (Helen died in late November 1998) was fond of saying when describing Tower Hill, "All that happens here is like manna from Heaven."

In a departure from this narrative, I'd like to recognize the following groups and individuals for their financial, professional and visionary contributions to the Orangerie:

Louise I. Doyle for diverting a generous portion of the estate of her sister, Marjorie Doyle Rockwell, to the construction of the Orangerie, and her personal gift towards improvements in the Stoddard Education and Visitors Center directed by her dear friend Allen Collachicco. Louise kept a watchful eye on the two-year design process and the year of construction.

Homsey Architects, Inc. of Wilmington, Delaware for designing this fine building and for faithfully and respectfully following the Master Plan and connecting the Orangerie to the Stoddard Center. Leonard Sophrin, Principal, and Curtis Harken, Associate.

Consigli Construction, Inc., of Milford, Massachusetts for so carefully putting all the pieces of this complicated puzzle together. Anthony Consigli, Jr., President, and Larry O'Brien, Project Supervisor.

Howard Peterson, Jr., who, undaunted, guided the Building Committee through the early stages of design, and who dependably followed and supported the building process.

Marco Polo Stufano, who chaired the Orangerie Committee, a fine committee of greenhouse managers, who gave guidance to the architects regarding the needs of plants (and how form follows function).

Louise Doyle breaks ground for the Orangerie, 1997.
The Orangerie was completed in 1999 (see pp. 102-103)

A Garden of People

Frank Callahan, master carpenter and apprentice to Andres Le Notre, gardener to Louis XIV of France, who "out Versailles-ed" Versailles.

Nancy Grimes, whose great appreciation and knowledge of eighteenth-century English lead cisterns, led to the donation and installation of these beautiful objects, and who, with sculptor Jane White, designed the handsome fountainheads.

John D. Mapel, Horticulturist, who conscientiously and creatively amassed a fine collection of plants and kept them alive under less than ideal conditions.

All of them and many others deserve a round of applause. No project this unique is possible without the interest and support of many far-thinking people.

And no occasion was complete without the commemorative poetic stylings of George Bernardin.

A PALM TREE'S LAMENT

Long ago and far away…
This little palm tree first saw—the light of day.
Under warm and sunny skies…
Where pelicans chase the butterflies.
My seed was planted near a sandy beach…
Above the highest tidal reach.
The winds were gentle and rains were mild…
As I grew into a handsome, healthy, palm-child,
No unmet needs—no worldly strife…
A place to grow for the rest of one's life.
But alas this was not to be…
Let me tell you what became of me.
It began one day when two smelly hicks…
Entered the field with shovels and picks.
They chopped and dug and let out some hoots…
As they severed and mangled my tender roots.
And at last a very nasty old hag…
Stuffed my bottom into a burlap bag.

They picked me up—and it was my luck...
To be shoved into the rear of a big, dark truck.
Woe is me, woe is me...
The driver looked like Simon Legree.
The boss gave him a great big bill...
To drive his truck to Tower Hill.
Soon it began to be somewhat chilly...
I began to feel like a worn out filly.
From time to time the driver stopped at a liquor store...
And paid a visit to a local whore.
On and on went his fiendish mission...
From bouncing and jouncing there was no remission.
At long last, we pulled onto French Drive...
I was barely, just barely alive.
They dumped me out on the cold, cold ground...
Trexler and his henchmen were just hanging around.
Soon a guy, as mean as a fox...
Dumped my roots into a big green box.
And into the container they poured sand and some loam...
This was, you see, to be my new home.
They pulled me inside a big glass shed...
And soaked me with water and had me fed.
At last I was here, in misery...
Growing in the so-called "Orangerie."
Pretty soon came opening day...
Men and ladies in fine array.
I had to endure one little weenie...
Who into my box poured a watered-down martini.
And an old dame with a whale of a nerve...
Who into my soil pushed a moldy hors d'oeuvre.
So, its no wonder I almost died...
My fronds all yellow and nearly dried.
But maybe my health will recover this Spring...
And I'll get used to this—*Orangerie* thing.

A Garden of People

In October of 1999, WCHS President Dale Harger received a letter from Louise Doyle regarding the naming of the Orangerie on January 29, 2049. Louise had wanted to name the Orangerie in my honor but the trustees felt it inappropriate to name the structure after the current living director. Leave it to Louise to come up with an alternative plan. In the library vault there is a plaque, a menu, and an acceptance speech from me in the likely event that I will be dead by 2049.

Camellias

We had many horticultural goals for the Orangerie but the display of three plant groups was paramount: palms, citrus, and camellias. The palms and citrus had been acquired in Florida but the camellias were a different story. The camellias, which are now primarily in the Limonaia, originated from three distinct collections: the Tower Hill collection, which were newer varieties, the Thayer Collection, and the Isabella Stewart Gardner Collection.

Nathaniel Thayer Dexter bequeathed his grandmother's (Ruth Simpkins Thayer) collection of camellias that was cultured at her Hawthorne Hill estate in Lancaster, Massachusetts, to the Worcester County Horticultural Society. Ruth Thayer's head gardener, William Anderson, who had been an officer of WCHS, bred some of the dozen or so plants gifted to Tower Hill.

In 1989, we were approached by Catha Rambus, director of the Wave Hill Catalog of Landscape Records, at the Wave Hill Gardens in the Bronx, about the fate of the Gardner Camellia Collection housed in the old conservatories of Isabella's "country place" in Brookline, Massachusetts. The conservatories were slated to be demolished to make room for a new house. It was suggested that we could come and dig the plants and move them into the Orangerie—NOT. Instead we took cuttings of each plant and started new vigorous plants grown in decorative containers. None of the specimens in question had a cultivar name attached. The best solution was to write a detailed description of each. Walter Hunnewell, a renowned horticulturist from Wellesley,

Massachusetts, did this as a favor to us and the Arnold Arboretum, who had also agreed to take cuttings. When all was said and done, we ended up with several plants from the ten or so Gardner plants. As far as attaching names, we thought we might be able to identify them from books written at the time the plants were first acquired by Isabella Stuart Gardner. This was not one hundred percent the case. The plants continue to thrive in the Orangerie and Limonaia.

A succession of projects followed the opening of the Orangerie and were under the Phase III umbrella: the naming of the Lawn Garden, the Entry Garden, the Systematic Garden (major gifts from Nadeau, Farber, Ciborowski, Thurston and Doyle), the Inner Park (major gifts from Bigelow, Jay and Pappas), Pliny's Fountain, Wildlife Refuge Pond (major gifts from Spear, Sudbury, Fuller and Fidelity Investments), and the Moss Steps.

Naming of the Lawn Garden

There was no kinder and gentler supporter of Tower Hill than Nathaniel Thayer Dexter whose family had been involved with WCHS since the 1920s. "Nat" served as a trustee and treasurer of the Horticultural Society for many years. When Nat died in July of 1999, he left the Society a legacy of more than one million dollars. We felt that the family was entitled to a memorial naming opportunity. Without hesitation they chose the Lawn Garden, which up to that point had no name. Nat never met a plant he didn't like and was particularly fond of the tree and shrub collection displayed in the Lawn Garden. On the occasion of Nat's birthday on May 14, 2000, with family gathered, the Lawn Garden became the "Nathaniel Thayer Dexter Lawn Garden."

---- CHAPTER SEVEN ----

Honor Roll

Systematic Garden

On the 1988 version of the Master Plan, the area that is currently the Systematic Garden was initially planned to be two gardens divided by a panel of grass. One was to be a perennial garden, the other a rose garden. As WCHS was approaching Phase III development, we began to rethink these themes. It was our intention to incorporate roses and perennials, where appropriate, throughout the Tower Hill landscape. After seeing the attractively designed Order Beds at Kew Gardens in London, I suggested the design of a systematic garden—a garden of plant evolution—in place of the original themes. The trustees agreed.

Because of their stellar work on the Entry Garden and siting of the Orangerie, Halvorson was awarded the contract to design the Systematic Garden. Blair Hines had left to start his own firm and we were assigned another designer. As hard as I tried, I could not work with this new person. We decided to sever our ties with Halvorson and contract with Blair. It proved to be a wise decision.

Above: Juneberry (*Amelanchier x grandiflora* cv. 'Ballerina')

The objective of the Systematic Garden was to display the evolution of plants from algae to angiosperms and everything inbetween, a garden of both botany and ornament. The definition of a plant?—an organism containing chlorophyll which can photosynthesize, absorbing carbon dioxide and emitting oxygen.

Algae, the oldest plant on earth, is a one-cell plant and multiplies through cell division. Moss and liverworts are next on the path of evolution. These are terrestrial plants with no roots, no stems and no leaves, but they do have spores for reproduction. Ferns and their allies appear tens of thousands of years later, supporting roots, stems, leaves, and spores. At one time there were fern trees in excess of one hundred feet.

In the next thousands of years came the gymnosperms, cycads and ginkgo; they have roots, trunks, stems, leaves, and seeds but no flowers. Flowering plants appeared in another hundred thousand years. These make up the primary display in the Systematic Garden. Divided into two types, monocots (flowering plants whose seeds typically contain only one embryonic leaf or *cotyledon*), and dicots (flowering plants whose seeds have two *cotyledons*), they are exhibited in parallel beds to illustrate their evolution in time frames parallel to one another.

The twenty-four or so flowering plant families in the garden are arranged chronologically starting with the magnolia and buttercup families and terminating to the north with the aster family. Understanding plant evolution is basic to human education. That the Systematic Garden is both educational and ornamental is a credit to the staff of Tower Hill.

The boundaries of the Systematic Garden were set by Pliny's Allée to the west, Orangerie to the south, pit house to the east and woodland to the north. The interpretation of the garden began in the Fern Gallery and progressed north to the edge of the existing woodland. It was our intention to show visitors the path of plant evolution all the way from the one-celled algae to the complex and efficient dandelion.

Blair designed the garden in the Italian Renaissance style, with a series of beds, fountains and structures. The plant families most important to daily human life were assigned to particular beds and, as stated, were arranged from oldest to most advanced.

Honor Roll

It's About Time!

The Systematic Garden's Lesson of How Plants Evolved on Earth

Timeline of the Evolution of Plant Life on Our Planet

Present   FIRST HUMANS APPEAR 20,000 YEARS AGO
Quaternary
Modern Forests
1.65 million years ago
Tertiary
Flowering Plants diversify
(new research indicates that the diversification of flowering plants started 30 million years earlier than suspected — 90 million years ago)

65 million years ago
Cretaceous
Flowering Plants appear
146 million years ago
Jurassic
Cycads, Conifers, Gingkos flourish
Age of Dinosaurs
213 million years ago
Triassic
Conifers flourish
245 million years ago
Permian
Cycads, Gingkos appear
286 million years ago
Carboniferous
Giant Tree ferns, Horsetails flourish
First Conifers
360 million years ago
Devonian
First Seed-bearing Plants
Ferns, Horsetails, Clubmosses appear
Mosses appear
Silurian
First Land Plants
Cambrian
Primitive Seaweed
570 million years ago
Precambrian
1 billion years ago
Algae
3.5 billion years ago
Bacteria flourish
3.8 billion years ago
First life
4.5 billion years ago
Earth is formed

Humans are justifiably proud of their accomplishments in art, architecture, science and invention; it's difficult to even imagine a world without the human race. And yet, for most of Earth's history there were no people at all. Everything humans have created, from the first cave paintings to the tallest skyscrapers, happened in the last 20,000 years. Recorded history began only 8,000 years ago. This represents a mere "blink of an eye" compared to the long stretches of time when other organisms dominated the planet. All of human history, from man's appearance to your visit to Tower Hill today, is represented by a tiny sliver at the end of this timeline.

The earliest entities to be called "life" originated in the oceans 3.8 billion years ago. Simple, single-celled creatures that were neither plant nor animal, they were the only life on Earth for billions of years. Some of their close relatives survive today.

The first true plants, the **algae**, appeared in the oceans a billion years ago, flourishing for the next 500 million years. Many species of seaweed found in the ocean today are virtually identical to their ancestors. Eventually, some aquatic plants evolved internal systems to store water, enabling them to survive temporary dry periods, and they began to colonize the land. Evidence suggests that all land plants came from a single common ancestor that eventually developed into mosses and ferns.

Over the next hundred million years, land plants developed the ability to produce seeds. The **Gymnosperms** (cycads, gingkos and conifers) represent some of the oldest living examples of these.

During the next hundred million years, land plants developed even further, producing flowers and encasing their seeds in fleshy fruits. Today, these **Angiosperms** number about 300,000 different species, including most of the plants we are familiar with in our gardens.

The Systematic Garden traces the evolution of land plants from their appearance on Earth hundreds of millions of years ago to their present-day forms. Some of their adaptations for survival may be obvious, but some may surprise you. Explore the Systematic Garden to learn more about the surprising evolutionary path that land plants have taken to survive on earth.

Interpretive sign for the Systematic Garden showing the evolution of plants
Designed by Robert Zeleniak

The decorative details of the Systematic Garden were carefully thought out. Commemorative opportunities abounded and all had generous and appropriate price tags.

Swedish Urn and Benches

Two urns with flanking benches were sited on the southwest and northwest borders. The Swedish Urn was to the south, the Welsh Talbot Urn to the north. William Thurston from Harvard, Massachusetts, chose one of the benches ($5,000) near the Swedish Urn in memory of his wife Ginny, a former WCHS trustee, and then was inspired to name the Urn after Ginny as well ($20,000). Not liking the idea of a "stranger's bench" on the other side of the urn, he bought the commemoration for that bench as well. My role in this charming scenario was only to have the opportunities at hand.

Primordial Pool

The Primordial Pool is a striking water and fountain feature on the south terrace of the Systematic Garden. With a concept in mind, I teamed with Blair Hines to design and execute it. It turned out to be one of the most interesting and popular fountains at Tower Hill.

One winter's day in early 2000, friend Jesse Farber spoke to me about a commemorative gift for her late husband Dan, a renowned photographer. I kept a list of commemorative gifts in my coat pocket. As she reiterated her goal for the day, I pulled out the list and handed it to her. This struck her as funny. In her distinctive southern drawl she said, "You *are* organized." She bought the commemorative rights to the Primordial Pool ($50,000) then and there. The plaque reads:

> In Memory of Daniel Farber
> Nature was his God
> April 14, 2000

The Victorian Fountain in the Systematic Garden

Victorian Fountain Court

In 1986, Robert Cushman, retired CEO of the Norton Company in Worcester, gifted to WCHS a circa-1880, single tear, cast-iron Victorian fountain produced by J.W. Fiske and Company with an aquatic motif. Bob had seen it listed for sale by a Maine antique dealer. Before he purchased it he called to see if the Society wanted it. Yes indeed!

Bob cleaned and painted the fountain in the Victorian style, using multiple colors to reflect the nature of the carvings. Cranes were painted to look like cranes, water lilies to look like water lilies, etc.

We installed a round fiberglass pool to form the base of the fountain and later added a coping of bluestone. At first it was located in the field south of, and on axis with, the front door of the Farmhouse. An extension cord from an outside plug was used to power the pump. It sat there until we started construction of the Lawn Garden, then moved to the lawn adjacent to the old well house at the rear of the Farmhouse. There it was used as a planter. After Pliny's Allée was planted, we moved the pool and fountain to the end of the allée. An electric chord ran three hundred feet to power the fountain.

In 1999, with the help of Henry Ciborowski, we acquired the pool base of an authentic circa-1880 Fiske Victorian fountain that had been buried for decades in the stone and soil dump of the Rural Cemetery in Worcester. The basin had a motif similar to the fountain and was the correct diameter to accommodate the splash. Blair incorporated a planter on the center of the east-west and north-south axis of the Systematic Garden. Both the basin and fountain were painted a dark green color. Henry Ciborowski made a gift of $30,000 to support the final home of the fountain and basin. The Victorian Fountain Court was dedicated in honor of the Ciborowski Family in September 2000.

Kinship Arbor

Also designed by Blair, a pergola was incorporated on the far north axis of the Systematic Garden. The four corners of the structure would each anchor a plant family bed related to the nightshade order. The pergola consisted of sixteen cast iron columns supporting a steel latticed frame. Blair had located the columns at a salvage yard in Roxbury, Massachusetts, and he, Joann and I took a field trip to see if they were appropriate. The yard was a foul-smelling, poison ivy-riddled mess but the columns were magnificent. While Joann and I waited, Blair negotiated the acquisition of the columns from the salvage yard owners. As it turned out, they donated the columns to us as a tax deduction—Blair and his magic ways.

The pergola's location and the romantic nature of its design caught the imagination of Barbara Booth and she made a $50,000 gift towards the building of the structure. Barbara often used the word "kin" when discussing her all-important family and the pergola was named the "Kinship Arbor." It was dedicated September 8, 2000.

The Systematic Garden before planting, 1999

Construction of the Monocot pool

The Vincenza Seasons

Four locations on the east boundary of the Systematic Garden were designated for statues of the Four Seasons that would terminate the view on the subordinate east-west axis. "Julia Agrippina" stepped forward to fund the commission and purchase of the statues from a studio in Vincenza, Italy. She went ahead and approved designs that we never saw. The statues were chiseled from a soft limestone known as Vincenza stone. Agrippina also commissioned six large pedestals to hold the Seasons as well as the two large urns on the western border—also on the subordinate east-west axis.

When the Seasons arrived, we were a bit take aback—four chubby children with snub noses, holding the symbols of the seasons they represented. After being informed that they were in an early Italian Renaissance style, they began to grow on us.

One of the Vincenza Four Seasons statues

Russ Nadeau and Blair Hines in front of the Primordial Pool, 2000

The contract for the Systematic Garden was given to Schumacher Landscape Construction and the project proceeded smoothly. Blair came at least once a week to follow progress. Joann and I oversaw the day to day. Watching the progress was beyond exciting. Each bed was built to interpret one or two plant families and Joann's job was to acquire the appropriate plants.

With the help of many loyal volunteers, the planting began in July 2000. Karen worked long and hard on the detailed interpretive signs. At the eleventh hour with the dedication date looming, Dale Harger informed me that a gentleman represented by his law firm wanted to acquire the naming rights for the Systematic Garden. Russell Ward Nadeau agreed to make an endowment bequest of $500,000 for the maintenance of the garden. Such a "deal" was unprecedented. Initially, I was uncomfortable with this arrangement as we were giving commemorative rights for the entire garden based on faith in a future legacy. So many had already given so generously for the naming rights of the many details of the garden. The garden was named the "D. J. and Alice Shumway Nadeau Systematic Garden" on September 8, 2000. The Nadeau bequest was received in January of 2015. We had 2,700 visitors the weekend the garden officially opened.

We Hold these Truths to be Self-Evident

The following words were mounted on the south wall of the Great Hall in the Stoddard Education and Visitors Center:

> PLANTS PROVIDE US WITH ALL THE FOOD WE EAT
> AND ALL THE AIR WE BREATHE.

Plants are the most important organisms on earth. A botanic garden has the responsibility of making this clear to visitors. The gardens at Tower Hill were designed to delight but also to educate visitors and inspire them to nourish and sustain the natural world—so it, in turn, will nourish and sustain us.

Pliny's Fountain

As Blair Hines was overseeing the construction of the Systematic Garden, he was also engaged to design Pliny's Fountain at the north terminus of Pliny's Allée. The vision was to create a fountain that would originate from the earth; water would "magically" appear from an opening—like a geyser. The water would have a steady pulse and then erupt every half-hour or so. I was inspired by a fountain I had seen in a Toronto shopping mall.

True to form, Blair located an eighteenth-century well stone in a stone dump in Petersham, Massachusetts, owned by Jim Dowd who was implementing the stonework for the Systematic Garden. The price was $2,500 and I bought it for WCHS on the spot. The stone was delivered on a flatbed truck and slowly and carefully put in place with a crane.

Pliny's Fountain at the north terminus of Pliny's Allée

Unbeknownst to me, trustee Shirley Williams and her husband Peter saw the well stone in place and they fell in love with it. For $50,000 they bought the naming rights to honor a friend. Though called Pliny's Fountain, it is in memory of Henry Horner. The north vestibule, allée, and bench were named in memory of Pliny Allen, Barbara Booth's brother; the fountain and path were named to honor the Plinys of classical Rome. "Pliny's Bench" was custom made by Dovetail Woodworks of Worcester. It was gifted by Scott Ewing, a past treasurer of WCHS, and Pliny Allen's roommate at prep school. The fountain was dedicated on September 8, 2000.

Pliny's Path

Connecting the Belvedere to the west and the Inner Park to the east, is Pliny's Path. Its entire length cuts through native forest. The stretch of forest to the east was formerly the woodlot for the old farm, an area where the farmers preserved the forest, selectively thinning trees when there was a need for wood. The forest is also one of, if not the only, area at Tower Hill where there are remnants of American chestnuts, (*Castanea americana*).

Inner Park

In December 1998, the Bigelow family pledged $250,000 to name the Inner Park the "Palmer W. Bigelow, Jr. Inner Park." The family's patriarch and former president of Bigelow Nurseries had died earlier in the year. Palmer had a great appreciation for native plants and the family thought this a fitting tribute.

When the Bigelow family approached me about making a gift in Palmer's memory, my first thought was that they could choose a tree ($5,000) to be planted in the Inner Park. They responded that they were thinking of something "larger." I then suggested naming the Quarry Trail ($50,000) in the Inner Park. Again they said "no—something larger perhaps?"

"Well, there's the naming of the Inner Park itself," I offered.

That struck a chord.

$100,000 of their gift went towards the Palmer W. Bigelow Fund for the support of the Inner Park. The remainder of the gift was donated "in kind," the thinning and planting of trees and the proper dressing of the paths—a perfect partnership.

Folly

As the Bigelow Family addressed the naming of the Park, Worcester resident Tay Ann Jay was considering a memorial to her late husband Robert. A few years before, she had approached me about gifting a "folly." Tay, Sid Callahan and I had attended a lecture on Castletown, an estate garden in Wicklow, Ireland, that happened to have a folly.

"Would the Society consider a folly at Tower Hill?" Tay asked.

What could I say but "Of course."

Tay pledged a considerable amount, including a $10,000 endowment, for the construction of the Folly. Follies can take many forms and Tay chose the design of an ancient temple ruin. The location was to be the northwest corner of the Inner Park, up slope. Nancy Grimes of New England Garden Ornaments and Peter Deveikis, a.k.a. the "Stardust Twins," designed a four-columned porch sitting on a high plinth with a niche for a fountain.

I wanted to create a story around the Folly to give it a romantic anchor. Where to start? I envisioned the grottoed plinth built of Castalia stone, the same stone used for the Primordial Pool. The stairs and retaining walls in Helen Stoddard's garden were constructed with this type of stone and we were given the surplus by her daughters after Helen died. After years of Helen's references to this stone, I was curious enough to look up "Castalia:" first definition, "a town in Ohio," second definition, "a spring on Mt. Parnassus in Greece sacred to the God Apollo and the Muses, a source of inspiration." The Folly became the Temple of Apollo and the Muses. The muses were represented by the fountain, the Spring of Castalia—a good story.

Two members of Consigli Construction from Milford assembled the Folly. The four-columned porch was pristine when finished, however, and did not resemble an ancient structure that had suffered the ravages of time. That's where the Stardust Twins came in. With hammer and chisel they methodically chipped away at the structure, creating fissures in the columns and taking away the sharp edges, then staining the stone. When they had finished, the Folly looked two thousand-years-old. (See p. 106.)

Hercules Unchained and Wonder Woman

Early Sunday walks at Tower Hill became a routine for me and they invariably led me to the Inner Park. I chose different benches to sit and take in the stillness, sounds and fragrance of the woodland. One Sunday I approached the Park from the Meadow on the Loop Trail with a turn onto the Quarry Trail. There was a particular bench near the Friendship

Urn that I was fond of, maybe because the Urn was a gift from my dear friend Barbara Booth. I sat for at least five minutes before I became aware of activity at the Folly and then I did a double take. A man with longish black hair wearing overalls stood on the porch between the two central columns. Kneeling on the slope at the base of the Folly, a woman held a camera at the ready. I couldn't quite hear what I later assumed were her directions but the man unzipped his overalls and let them drop to his ankles, revealing that he was wearing nothing underneath. He stretched out his arms between the columns. Time passed, photos were taken, overalls readjusted. They gathered their paraphernalia and made their way down slope to where I was sitting. We smiled at one another and commented on the beauty of the day. They moved on. I resumed my walk through the park.

The following Sunday, I repeated my morning ritual. As I entered the Park on the Loop Trail from the Meadow, I saw something going on at the Temple of Peace. It was the same couple but this time the man was controlling the camera. The rather *zaftig* woman was posed on the table in the Temple, wearing a gold lamé bikini, diadem, and sandals. They barely acknowledged me until I mentioned that *perhaps* sitting on the table was unsafe and that *maybe* they should rethink Tower Hill as a backdrop for future photo shoots. I went on my way hoping that this would be the last encounter. It was.

Henry's Cupid

Other bits and pieces of stone and a column were located in association with the Temple. At the top of the column we placed a bronze cupid, a gift from Henry Ciborowski, the only statue at Tower Hill that was anatomically correct. It had originally sat on a table in the entrance to the Stoddard building. Its private parts received so much attention I thought it best to put it out of reach—where it could not be molested.

The Temple of Peace in the Inner Park, gift of Arthur and Martha Pappas

Temple of Peace

In 2001, Martha and Arthur Pappas approached me regarding the building of a monument in the Inner Park. This was fortuitous. I felt that the Park needed another structure to balance the visual weight of the Folly. The structure was to be located in the southeast quadrant of the Park. The $60,000 donation funded the purchase and assembly of the Temple of Love, and $40,000 went to endow its maintenance. We scheduled the temple installation for the summer of 2002 but in the interim, nearly 3,000 people lost their lives as a result of the terrorist attacks of 911. We decided that the monument should be a memorial to peace. The Temple of Peace was dedicated on August 25, 2002.

Frank Callahan building the gatehouse at the entrance to Tower Hill, 1992

Memorial to Frank Callahan. The inscription reads:

FRANCISVS CALLAHANVS (Frank Callahan)
AB URBE CONDITA (From the founding of the city, Rome in 753 bce)
MMDCLXXIII (2673) – MMDCCLVIII (2758)
AMICVS (Friend)

Honor Roll

Frank's Column

In the far south-central boundary of the Park, a fluted Corinthian column was erected on an inscribed base. Frank Callahan died in 2005 and friends funded this monument in his honor. After a brief dialog, Sid Callahan and I thought this type of memorial would appeal to Frank's interest in Greco-Roman history as well as compliment other memorials in the Park.

Trees

As much as the Inner Park is about the memorials, it is also about the trees and shrubs that inhabit it. The Park is a natural diverse ecosystem of oak, beech, maple, birch, hickory, pine, red cedar, blueberry, huckleberry, witch-hazel, viburnum, aronia, lycopodium and much more. In the process of installing the system of paths, we removed trees to allow sun to reach the forest floor. Opening up the area gave us opportunities to plant new and complimentary trees. Many of these also became commemorative and were locations for interment of cremated remains or "cremains."

The first memorial tree was a hybrid magnolia "Yellow Bird," It was planted to honor a boy nicknamed Yellow Bird who had died at the age of two. The second was a tulip tree (*Liriodendron tulipifera*), planted to honor Dr. Anne Nesbitt, whose daughter's favorite tree was the tulip tree. When Anne's cancer was diagnosed as terminal, she had the tree installed while she could enjoy it. We chose the location together.

Good friends Stefan Cover and Rosemary Monahan were also fans of Tower Hill. A remarkable plantsman, Stefan successfully propagated all but one species of magnolia native to the United States east of the Mississippi River. One beautiful Saturday morning, the three of us planted sturdy young trees of *Magnolia pyramidata, acuminata, fraseri, asheii, macrophylla, tripetala, and cordata*. Later we added *Magnolia virginiana*, a gift from the Morris Arboretum in Philadelphia. *Magnolia grandiflora* is espaliered on the north wall of the Orangerie.

Martha Pappas donated a pink mountain silverbell (*Halesia carolina*) south of the Temple of Peace in honor of a friend. A so-called disease resistant American chestnut (*Castanea dentata*) was planted to honor Phyllis Stoddard, long-time Development Coordinator at Tower Hill. Eventually succumbing to blight, it was replaced in 2015 with an eastern redbud (*Cercis canadensis*).

Oh So Personal—and Not

In 2000, I took two trips, one to Cleveland the other to San Francisco. In Cleveland I received the Mrs. Oakley Thorne Medal for outstanding achievement in garden design at the annual meeting of the Garden Club of America. The presenter went on to say: "Presented to John W. Trexler, who in only fifteen years, designed, relocated and built Massachusetts' Tower Hill Botanic Garden into New England's most comprehensive botanic garden and a major center for horticultural education." This was indeed a great honor.

My trip to San Francisco could not have been more different. My mother actually knew the place and date of my conception—yes, my conception—the St. Francis Hotel, Tuesday, November 14, 1950. I made arrangements with friends in San Jose, to come for a short stay and to have cocktails at the St. Francis on Tuesday, November 14, the fiftieth anniversary of that twinkle in my mother's eye. They thought this to be an odd but novel idea for a celebration. At 6:30 p.m. we raised our gin martinis and toasted my "special celebration." Too much information?

Wildlife Pond

In January 1999, the month the Orangerie was dedicated, Ivan Spear, husband of past WCHS president Hope Spear, decided to make a gift of $200,000 in honor of Hope, who was gravely ill. Thinking fast, I suggested the Wildlife Pond as an appropriate project. Hope had always loved the Wildlife Garden. He agreed that the Pond would be a "fitting memorial."

The dedication of the Wildlife Pond in memory of Hope Spear, 2002

On the Master Plan, the pond was actually drawn as a series of ponds, comprising approximately three acres of water surface. Geoff Rausch assumed the ponds would be sustained by artificial means. By the mid-nineties, due to water shortages, we were determined to sustain the pond, which was now planned to be singular, by natural runoff. Working with the Boylston Conservation Commission, we eventually settled on a half-acre site in the Meadow Garden, just "a bit off" the central east-west axis of the Systematic Garden. Being axially obsessed, this drove me nuts until I realized that placing an octagonal viewing pavilion on the axis line at the edge of the pond would tie everything together nicely.

In the development of Tower Hill, each garden had three specific approaches: horticultural, interpretive and decorative. For example, the Wildlife Pond was to consist of indigenous wetland plants, illustrate watershed and the accommodation of the flow of water from Tower Hill, and display a rustic architectural style. The Inner Park consisted of native North American woodland plants, illustrated forest succession, and displayed the style of an eighteenth-century English Park.

Blair Hines was hired to design the pond and to site the pavilion and rustic overlook. David Robinson from New Jersey designed, built and installed the structures. I wrote the interpretive panels which Bob Zeleniak designed and produced. Joann and crew planted the perimeter of the pond with over eight hundred native shrubs.

The Wildlife Pond was dedicated on May 17, 2002. We set up a podium and some chairs on the adjacent Loop Trail. Dale Harger, president at the time, Ivan Spear and I each gave speeches. When it was Ivan's turn, he approached the podium carrying a large briefcase. He opened it and took out a frighteningly thick collection of paper. Everyone quietly gasped, dreading the speech that was to ensue. As far as I was concerned, he could speak as long as he wanted; it was his day. Well, it turned out he had set us up with a visual joke. He said a few kind words about his wife Hope and Tower Hill and then invited everyone back to the Farmhouse for drinks and food.

At the same time, we dedicated the Rustic Overlook in honor of the Fidelity Foundation and the Sudbury Foundation, both of whom had consistently supported Tower Hill development. They had liked the concept of the Wildlife Pond. The viewing pavilion was dedicated in honor of the Fuller Foundation. The Nesting Island honored Isabel Arms. A bench was named for Clayton Fuller, a member of the Boylston Conservation Commission, who died before the pond was completed. An American sycamore (*Platanus occidentalis*) was planted in memory of Cynthia Ann Moriarty-Schieven and a silver maple (*Acer saccharinum*) in memory of Mary Spahr. Both women had strong ties to Tower Hill.

Moss Steps

After Helen Stoddard died in November of 1998, her daughters, Judy King and Val Loring, settled her estate. In the process of going through Helen's papers, they found a note instructing them to approach me about the acquisition of an "Aeolian" or wind harp (Aeolius was king of the winds in Roman mythology). An Aeolian harp is large and sculptural

Honor Roll

The Moss Steps in memory of Helen Stoddard, given by her daughters, Val Loring and Judy King

and makes eerie sounds when the wind blows. I politely declined the harp and suggested that a more fitting memorial to their mother might be the recreation of the famous Moss Steps, designed by Fletcher Steele, which had been removed from Helen's garden when the property was sold. I had a location in mind in the off chance that the steps could be recreated at Tower Hill. Well, as Helen would say, *manna from heaven*—the steps were dropped in our lap.

   I took Val and Judy for a walk and showed them a slope that divided the planned Shade Garden from the Rock Garden (coincidentally, the feature on the Master Plan that most intrigued Helen). The location at Tower Hill faced southwest and Helen's original steps had also faced southwest. The degree and length of slope of the two sites were virtually identical. I contacted Blair, who contacted Jim Dowd, and they came up with a budget. An irrigation company provided an estimate to run a waterline from the Farmhouse to the proposed site of the steps. Moss needs lots of water. A budget was presented and approved.

Like the originals, the new steps would be made of Castalia stone. We had a stockpile left from the building of the Primordial Pool. Working from a color photo of Helen's steps by renowned garden photographer Ken Druse, Blair engineered the Tower Hill version. He included a bluestone patio at the base and a two-riser stair to a path that proceeded to the future Rock Garden, ran along the southern end of the Shade Garden and led to the west entry of the Shade Garden from the Nuttery. Blair worked his magic. Val and Judy were more than pleased. To encourage the growth of moss, we did two things: pulverized and made a thick slurry of moss water and poured it on all the treads and poured beer on the treads. I learned both methods from Helen. The steps were dedicated September 7, 2002 (what would have been Helen's ninety-eighth birthday) in memory of Helen E. Stoddard.

Chinese Gate

The Shade Garden was developing an Asian theme with the Moss Steps and acquisition of a Japanese lantern. One particular day, I received a call from Bill Kitchen, Boylston resident and member of Tower Hill. He wanted to show me something that would be "perfect for Tower Hill." He led me to his spectacularly clean basement where a complete set of Chinese porcelain roofing tiles for a Chinese gate were arrayed on the floor. Bill had acquired the tiles from the same manufacturer who made replacement tiles for the Forbidden City in Beijing. He had hoped to erect the gate in his own garden but a family decision to move to Santa Barbara, California, put the "kibosh" on that dream. The tiles were spectacular and "the cookies were being passed," so yes, we would be happy to accept them. Bill wrapped and boxed the tiles; Steve and crew brought them to Tower Hill and stored them in the Orangerie basement. My goal was to have the gate constructed between the barway leading into the Asian woods from the Nuttery path. The width of the gate was eleven feet, the width of the barway just over eleven feet. I subtly started identifying a donor, but was unsuccessful before I retired. The tiles still wait patiently in the cellar of the Orangerie.

Honor Roll

A Note on Phase III

Phase III formally ended in summer of 2002. We raised a total of 7.3 million dollars and we spent $60,000 to raise that amount, less than .82% of the total. This labor of fundraising love was all done in house.

Master Plan for Buildings

Leonard Sophrin, the lead architect on the design of the Orangerie, left Homsey and established a private practice in Wilmington, Delaware. Before the Orangerie was dedicated, Lenny approached us regarding a Master Plan for Buildings. He felt we had a very good master plan for the property, but didn't have as clear picture of what would be our future building needs. In May 2000, the board unanimously voted to hire Lenny to guide us through the process of creating a Master Plan for Buildings.

The Master Plan Committee walked through every interior space at Tower Hill to fully understand what we had before assessing what we needed and also to determine what Phase IV would be. An essential part of the planning process was to develop an organizational chart to determine staff and office needs. It would also serve the purpose of prioritizing existing and future offerings such as library and archives, garden shop, food service, interior horticultural displays, exhibitions and flower shows, rentals/weddings, administrative, development and education offices. This task was assigned to the Personnel Committee with input from trustees and staff.

The plan suggested the acquisition of two parcels of land: the remaining frontage on Tower Hill Road, which would give us control of the road and use of it as a service/emergency drive, and Bob's and my property at 16 School Street, Maple Grove, which would be used for staff housing and as a small public garden. Both properties came on the market in 2014. Neither were purchased by the Society.

The original concept of a building quadrangle was still determined to be our best option. Lenny generated a schematic floor plan of the completed quadrangle, framing an interior courtyard or Winter Garden. His recommendations were to:

1. Move library to main floor of new east wing. Turn east half of existing library to two classrooms, west half to education offices, and axial center into a connecting north/south hallway.
2. Convert Mezzanine storage into administrative and development offices.
3. Reorient entrance to gift shop to the east
4. Reestablish Great Hall as reception, exhibition and rental space.

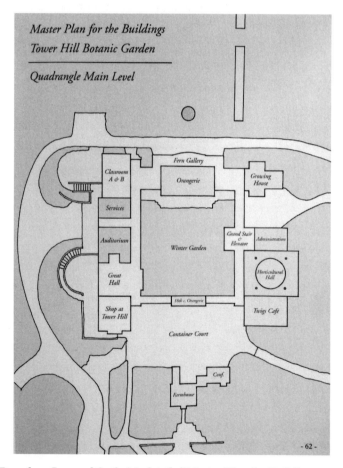

Page from Leonard Sophrin's detailed Master Plan for Buildings, 2003

5. Build new south wing to contain an expanded reception area adjacent to gift shop.
6. Build Limonaia to reflect a similar use as Orangerie on axis with the Orangerie and Farmhouse.
7. Build a southeast link connected to restaurant and east gallery
8. Build new east wing to support the restaurant, 4000+ sq. ft. exhibition/rental hall, new library, volunteer space, and gallery connecting to existing northeast link and Orangerie. This would create a 360-degree winter promenade through lush horticultural display.

Early in 2002, Lenny's Master Plan for Buildings was unanimously accepted. We also asked Lenny to recommend architects capable of generating plans for Phase IV. Top on his list was Centerbrook Architects from Centerbrook, Connecticut. They were on the job by December of the same year with instructions to develop a design for the completed quadrangle and set a realistic budget.

FINANCES

When I arrived at the Worcester County Horticultural Society in 1984, the annual budget was less than $200,000, the endowment a modest $250,000. When I left in 2011, the budget was 2.2 million, the endowment a healthy fifteen million. In the early years, managing the daily operation was quite simple. Rental of the horticultural hall at 30 Elm Street for wedding receptions, concerts, dancing lessons and parties was the primary source of income, along with membership dues, gate receipts from flower shows, grants from local foundations and donations. Maintaining the 25,000-square-feet Horticulture Building was the largest expense, then salaries which were modest. Administering these early budgets was a shared task between an administrative assistant and me.

By 1986, things had changed. We worked closely with the treasurer of the board of trustees. Three memorable treasurers were Henry Rudio,

Scott Ewing, and Allen Krause. Henry was a CPA with Main Hurdman, Scott an owner of several regional Hallmark stores, and Allen was the retired CFO of Memorial Hospital. Henry brought us into the age of computers and organized our accounting system. Scott, with the assistance of Jean Jones (Harger), built upon what Henry had started and took the reins in endowment management. Allen took the job seriously and was focused on an array of specific reports. This kept the financial managers very busy anticipating and fulfilling his requests. With such competent leadership, I was able to take a laissez faire approach to the finances and stay focused on the projects and raising funds to assure their success.

During my tenure as executive director, I had the good fortune to work with two outstanding financial managers as part of my staff: Pat duFosse from Northborough and Sharon Chauvin from Douglas. Pat and her successor Sharon capably wrapped their arms around the many layers of the Society's finances. There was the operating budget, income and expenses. There was also the capital budget and the varied restricted funds. My only bone of contention was the decision to combine, in terms of reporting, the draw down of the restricted funds—most of which I had established—with the draw down of the unrestricted funds. I felt that the two are very different and should remain separate.

Sick as a Dog #1

On April 12, 2002, while strolling through the Inner Park and Wildlife Garden with Kathleen Davis, our Development Coordinator (she was hired after Phyllis Stoddard retired), I began having shortness of breath and chest pains. Kathleen insisted I call my doctor who sent me straight to the emergency room at Memorial Hospital in Worcester. I was admitted and treated as if I was having a heart attack. I was eventually diagnosed with pericarditis, an inflammation of the pericardium, the membrane enclosing the heart. A cardiologist, a pulmonologist and a rheumatologist eventually determined that I suffered from psoriatic arthritis. I have been treated for this chronic disease ever since.

CHAPTER EIGHT

A Garden Within Reach

Phase IV

Centerbrook Architects and Planners was hired in late 2002 to flesh out Lenny Sophrin's schematic recommendations for the completion of the Quadrangle. It was determined that Phase IV would include the completed buildings as well as the Winter Garden, Herb Garden, Physic Garden, and Container Court. Since gardens were such an integral part of the phase, we made the decision to hire Melissa Marshall from Marshall Tyler, who had been part of the original master planning team, Environmental Planning and Design, in 1986.

Although Phase IV was the priority and I was focused on working closely with Centerbrook, I was juggling other major projects. One was a feasibility study of wind-generated power at Tower Hill. We named the study the "Aeolian Project" in recognition of Aeolius, king of the winds in Roman mythology. The Kendall Foundation awarded WCHS a grant for the feasibility study. The conclusion was: Yes—we have steady winds at Tower Hill but the cost of erecting a wind turbine would be

Above: Hiba cedar (*Thujopsis dolabrata* var. *hondae*)

prohibitive—more than $500,000 plus an additional $5000 annual maintenance cost. We were not eligible for any government grants and the price tag far exceeded any savings we would realize. We had done our due diligence and were able to pull out the study when—every few years—a trustee would inevitably suggest a wind turbine.

Marillyn's Piano

In December 2004, Marillyn (yes, two "l's") Zacharis, a new and interested trustee who had been introduced to WCHS by Susan Dumaine, approached me about gifting a grand piano to Tower Hill. Did I think it was needed? "When the cookies are being passed …"

We made a date to go to M. Steinert and Sons, Boston's premier piano dealer, to look and listen—and not necessarily buy. We met with a

Marillyn Zacharis choosing the grand piano at M. Steinert and Sons

sales person and listened to a Boston grand piano with an approximate $35,000 price tag. We liked what we heard, but for kicks and giggles (knowing how expensive they were), we also listened to a Steinway grand. There was no comparison. I looked at Marillyn; she looked at me, and we silently acknowledged the better instrument. Marillyn didn't hesitate. She bought the Steinway—twice the price of the Boston. She also purchased a trolley for moving the piano from room to room and she pledged an additional five thousand dollars a year to maintain the piano and subsidize recitals. She would later pledge $100,000 for a fund she named the "Marimuse Fund" for the support of the piano and recitals. We celebrated with lunch at the Four Seasons nearby on Boylston Street.

An inaugural concert was held on February 15, 2005 with Ken Wolf as performer. Ken was a research scientist who had been a piano prodigy. He was talented and popular and honored to perform on our new instrument. My one request was that the opening piece be W.A. Mozart's *Piano Sonata #16 in C major K. 545*. It was the first piece of classical music I remembered at the age of fourteen. The remainder of the program was all Beethoven. Marillyn was applauded for her generosity, Ken for his exquisite performance.

That same winter, we hired Boylston architect Jonathan Richmond to design an accessible connection between the meeting room and the main part of the Farmhouse. His design was brilliant and well-received by the Boylston Planning Board. Consigli Construction agreed to build it for the cost of materials. Howard Peterson of Peterson Oil in Worcester installed an HVAC system at no cost. Barbara Booth gave $33,000 for the renovation (she would later donate another $47,000 to replace all the Farmhouse windows). Tay Ann Jay donated a set of Rosenthal dinnerware and supported the renovation with a gift of $30,000. Julia Agrippina gave ten place settings of Gorham sterling flatware.

In 2005 the trustees concluded that completing the quadrangle was more than WCHS could tackle in this phase. They did agree to expanding the entrance, reorienting the entrance to the gift shop, building the Limonaia and the southeast link, and building a series of storage and mechanical rooms off what was called the "cryptoporticus." They also approved the regrading of the service road on the west side of the Stoddard Building to make it true to the original 1988 design. And finally they gave the go ahead for the construction of the Winter Garden and the Container Court. This was certainly enough to take on. We called it Phase IVA, the assumption being that Phase IVB would be the completion of the Quad, the Herb Garden and Physic Garden.

In 2004, we had a sense of what the Winter Garden with its central pool was going to look like. Kitty Ferguson pledged $500,000 towards

The original atrium pool in Domitian's palace in Rome, Italy

"Domitian's Pool." Julia Agrippina had wanted the naming rights to the pool but Kitty beat her to it. Instead, Julia pledged one million for the construction of the Winter Garden itself and five million towards endowment. Chloe Sundberg donated $100,000 to commission the fountains in Domitian's Pool. These three remarkable women initiated the capital drive for Phase IVA.

The original vision was for Domitian's Pool to function, not only as a decorative garden pool, but also as an aquarium. This meant it would have to be at least nine feet in depth. A subterranean room would exist beneath the Winter Garden accessed from the Horticultural Hall vestibule and portholes in the pool superstructure would allow visitors to observe fish and aquatic plants. This concept intrigued Kitty. After a fiscal reality check, the aquarium idea was abandoned. The pool became a standard eighteen inches deep with a heated floor to assure the function of the fountains in winter. The pool's outline was inspired by an atrium pool in Domitian's palace (Domus Augustana) on the Palatine Hill in Rome.

A Wonderful Connection

I became good friends with both Kitty Ferguson and her sister Louise Riemer. In a roundabout way, I learned that they were related to the Lincoln and Davis families of Worcester whom Louise joked "... were probably from the wrong side of the tracks." Truth be known, you're definitely not from the wrong side of the tracks if you're a Lincoln or a Davis from Worcester.

Isaac Davis and Daniel Waldo Lincoln, Kitty and Louise's great great grandfathers, were two of the six founders of the Worcester County Horticultural Society. Three other important nineteenth-century WCHS players, also connected to Kitty and Louise, were Governor John Davis, uncle to Isaac, Daniel Waldo, uncle to Daniel Lincoln, and Edward Winslow Lincoln, nephew to Daniel Lincoln. What a wonderful coincidence that these two ladies became such an important part of the Tower Hill story ... or was it?

Sisters Louise Riemer and Kitty Ferguson

As phase IV was in the planning stages, I wrote an interpretive sign explaining the goals of the phase with the headline "Nice and Easy Wins the Race," referencing Aesop's fable, *The Tortoise and the Hare*. The fable complimented Augustus Caesar's motto *Festina Lente*—"Make Haste Slowly" (which had to do with military strategy), a favorite of Julia Agrippina's. This led to the idea of twin tortoises as fountain sculptures in Domitian's Pool. Chloe Sundberg loved the idea of donating the funds for an original work of art and Priscilla Deichman was commissioned to create the bronze fountains. She was renowned as a sculptor of animals and produced works for the Bronx Zoo in New York and the National Zoo in Washington, D.C. Her grandfather was Rene Paul Chambellans, famed Art Deco sculptor. The apple did not fall far from the tree.

Priscilla had previously created a life-size bronze of the native eastern box turtle. Since she was already familiar with their physiology, she suggested our tortoises be box turtles at five times scale. Architect Melissa Marshall determined the size of the pool and the scale of the turtles

A Garden Within Reach

Chloe Sundberg and sculptor Priscilla Deichman discuss a model of the tortoise fountains for Domitian's Pool.

Testing the fountains, 2010

in relation to it. When they were positioned, I suggested to Chloe that she might want to give them names. Her first thought was "Romulus and Remus" but I reminded her that Romulus had murdered his twin. I recounted to Chloe the story of two other twins: Castor and Pollux—how Castor was born mortal to Leda and the king of Sparta and Pollux was born immortal to Leda and Zeus. (Their sister was Helen of Troy). Castor was killed in battle and Pollux asked his father if he could share his immortality with his brother. Zeus was so touched by the request that he made them both immortal and created the constellation Gemini in their honor. The turtle to the north that hides the pump is Pollux and the one to the south is Castor. But sometimes they're simply referred to as the "Turtle Boys."

At the same time that the turtle fountains were being created, we worked with Nancy Grimes on the design of four Roman agricultural deity statues for display in the Winter Garden, flanking the north and south

Christian Primeau and Joann Vieira prepare Proserpina for dedication.

stairs. Adopted as symbols by the Horticultural Society in 1842, the specific deities were: Flora, goddess of flowers and spring, Ceres, goddess of agriculture, Pomona, goddess of the orchard, and Vertumnus, god of the orchard and Pomona's soulmate. We added a fifth, Proserpina, daughter of Ceres. Nancy suggested that the sculptures be cast in Coade stone, a durable twice-baked terracotta developed by Eleanor Coade in the eighteenth century. We placed a commemorative value of $100,000 on each statue. Flora and Proserpina were quickly snapped up, the former by Julia Agrippina, the latter by Chloe Sundberg and they arrived within the year. The remaining three were not purchased. Because the pedestals did not turn out to be winter hardy, the two statues were eventually displayed in the Orangerie.

Sick as a Dog #2

In April 2007, my rheumatologist became concerned about a bad cough I had developed. After receiving a chest x-ray, I noticed that the technician was keeping his distance. He said he hoped I would be "okay." Strange. I heard nothing more from my doctor and called the following Monday. She had not had time to look at the x-ray. When she did, she sent me straight to a pulmonologist who had me hospitalized with tuberculosis-like symptoms. I was isolated for nine days, attended by an infectious disease doctor and put on a six-month regimen of drugs.

The WCHS trustees hired a consultant to develop a succession plan in preparation for my eventual retirement—or death.

Highlights of the spring of 2007 were:

1. Centerbrook Architects presented a new estimate of $8 million for Phase IVA.

2. We began construction on an expansion of the north end of the Stoddard Center, giving us prep-space for classrooms A and B and the Orangerie, and the addition of closets in A and B.

3. We graded the area designated to be the future Vegetable Garden.

4. The Mezitt family of Weston Nursery pledged $250,000 towards the Shade Garden/Asian Woods. They want to approach the project in the same manner as the Bigelow family addressed the Inner Park, gifts both monetary and "in kind." (It was a great honor to have such a distinguished family support Tower Hill in a thoroughly horticultural way).

5. An $8000 gift was received from the Yawkey foundation for the education of inner city teachers in plant science.

6. We were awarded a $675,000 grant from the Massachusetts Cultural Council for Phase IVA.

7. We received $200,000 from the Fidelity Foundation to support our technology plan.

8. We received a bequest of $107,000 from the estate of Clifford DeFlumear for scholarships.

9. Jean and Myles McDonough pledged $100,000 to Phase IVA.

10. Jennifer Saltonstall Cabot donated two spectacular Sergeant weeping hemlocks to flank the main Loop Trail entrance to the Inner Park in memory of Kitty Ferguson.

The Loop Trail

Strategically, the Loop Trail was the most important feature on the Master Plan. A mile in length, the trail is more "road" than trail. Its circulation gives it direct contact with the Lawn Garden, Orchard, Dry Garden, Fruit Garden, Nuttery, Vegetable Garden, Herb Garden, Physic Garden, Container Court, Systematic Garden, Field Garden, Inner Park, Meadow Garden, Wildlife Pond and Garden, Shade Garden and Rock Garden. It is intended to be a measured walk as well as a tram circuit for visitors. Its most easterly circuit is a portion of the eighteenth-century farm road.

Norman's Rock

Early in the development of the Loop Trail, we hired a young man named Norman to widen and level the trail with a bulldozer. Norman was eager and willing. After I gave him instructions, I left him to his own devices.

An exposed stone in the trail had created a slight hump which could have been left in place and easily addressed with a small amount of fill. Norman, however, saw this stone as a personal challenge. Common sense ceased to function. He methodically and skillfully maneuvered his "dozer" (a *bull*dozer, mind you, not a backhoe) to extract this obstacle from the trail. When I returned a few hours later, an enormous boulder sat to one side and in the middle of the trail was an even larger hole. Norman had a proud grin on his face. I was at a loss for words.

Norman managed to fill and compact the hole properly and "Norman's Rock" is a landmark along the Loop Trail—also a good opportunity for a story during garden tours.

It's rare that a foundation comes knocking on your door to suggest you make an application for funding. The 1772 Foundation, whose primary mission is the preservation of antique houses and heritage farmlands, was attracted to Tower Hill mainly due to the existence of the Preservation Orchard. After an in-depth walk, the foundation representatives developed an appreciation for the Children's Garden. At this point the Children's Garden was a gardening camp for children, five- to twelve-years-old, called the Farm School. A fence was needed to define the space and to discourage nuisance animals from entering planted areas. The 1772 Foundation financed the purchase and installation of a four-foot fence and four gates at the south, north, east and west ends of the large rectangular area.

One of our great disappointments in 2008 was the news that our one million dollar grant request to the Kresge Foundation was rejected. We had been successful with Kresge in Phases II and III and we were confident we would be successful a third time. *C'est la vie.*

On a beautiful early autumn day, I was at Marillyn Zacharis' home in Wellesley pruning shrubs and trees. She had bought my services at a fundraising event at Tower Hill a few weeks earlier. With pole saw in hand, I was removing a large branch from a crabapple tree as Marillyn assisted. As I methodically sawed, she brought up the disappointment of the Kresge grant. Changing the subject, she then lamented the fact that the commemorative rights to the Limonaia were two million dollars. Without skipping a stroke of the saw I said glibly, "Marillyn, for you, it's a mere million."

Just as fast, Marillyn responded, "I could do that."

Dumbfounded, I stopped sawing and said, "Really...?"

She would have to speak to her "money guy," and would get back to me the following Monday. Monday came; the pledge was secured. Hallelujah—*manna from heaven.*

And then more *manna*, we received an additional $500,000 from the estate of Julia Agrippina.

With the finances for Phase IVA in place, Betsy DeMallie, President of the Board, asked for a vote from the Executive Committee to proceed with construction. Six of the eight officers voted "yes" and two abstained. Marillyn, now a vice president, after having just pledged a million dollars sat there while two of her fellow officers abstained. I was bitterly disappointed for her and for the Society. Never in the history of Tower Hill had there been anything less than unanimous support for proceeding with a construction phase and never had so much money been raised for any one phase. Ironically, the two abstaining officers gave little in support of Phase IVA but seemed to have the loudest voices.

Barbara Booth at her home in Worcester
Courtesy of Greater Worcester Community Foundation
Photo by Dan Vaillancourt, 2006

BARBARA BOOTH

Our dear and generous friend Barbara Allen Booth suffered a stroke on May 27, 2009. She was placed in hospice care and died shortly thereafter. She was ninety-seven. A few months before her death, I made one of my many visits to her home at 7 Paul Revere Road in Worcester. We never had trouble finding things to discuss. On this particular visit we talked about the renewal of her membership to AARP. She had a choice to renew for one, three or five years. After some thought, she chose a three-year renewal. Her reasoning? She wanted to live to be a hundred. The Yankee in her probably still regrets the waste of money. She had a great sense humor and I miss her to this day.

By late summer 2009, we were well into construction of the west side of Phase IVA. Despite some hesitation to commit to all of IVA at once, the consensus was eventually to take on the "whole enchilada." Finances were secure.

Morgan Construction, a four-generation family owned manufacturing company in Worcester was sold and the Morgan family foundation pledged $500,000 to Phase IVA. Flip, former CEO of Morgan Worcester, and Gale Morgan, both longtime friends and supporters of WCHS, pledged an additional $75,000 to IVA. The new entry room at the Stoddard Education and Visitors Center was named the Morgan Entry Gateway.

Construction involved the installation of a new septic system, sized to accommodate the completion of the Quadrangle in Phase IVB. In lowering the west side road to allow street access to the Library and Classroom C, the west terrace had to be demolished and rebuilt. This also enabled the building of a delivery space, a new improved kitchen and a series of west to east rooms accommodating the computer server, kitchen and gift shop storage, bathroom, furnace room, and, at the far east end, a room that would plug into the future kitchen and restaurant and south-north exhibition hall and Library. Because this was important infrastructural development, I gave it the descriptive Latin title of *Cryptoporticus*, an underground walkway.

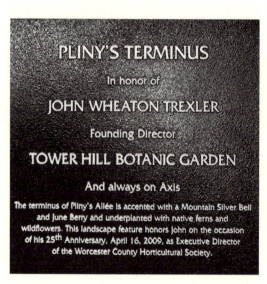

Plaque honoring John as Founding Director of Tower Hill
placed at the terminus of Pliny's Allée

During the flurry of early construction, the Society held a September celebration of my twenty-fifth anniversary as executive director which doubled as a fundraiser. The Society netted $104,000 for the elegant affair. $71,000 went towards an endowment to support the director's salary. A plaque was set into a boulder at the end of Pliny's Allée honoring me on the occasion of my anniversary and naming me the founding director of Tower Hill Botanic Garden. We used this celebratory weekend to open the Limonaia. The Limonaia was dedicated to Marillyn Zacharis and the Fuller Foundation. A general date of Autumn 2010 was applied.

The Limonaia is a solid, poured concrete structure with a decorative full brick skin on the exterior. The windows are triple hung and doors are French. The Limonaia, like all the gardens and structural features on the spine of the hill, is on axis with the central back door of the Farmhouse, though in the case of the Lawn Garden, on axis with the front door.

You never know where life will lead you ...
Or how I had a mild confrontation with Martha Stewart

On either side of the north doors of the Limonaia are a pair of concrete urns, a gift of Nancy Skinner, owner of the auction house Skinner, Inc. in Boston, in memory of her late husband Robert.

So the story begins.

After the dedication of the Orangerie in 1998, I was approached by Steve Fletcher, auctioneer and Vice President of Skinner which was then headquartered in Bolton, Massachusetts. Steve wanted to make me aware of a pair of urns stored behind Nancy Skinner's greenhouse in Bolton. He thought that Nancy would most likely gift them to the Horticultural Society if we were interested. Steve and I rendezvoused to take a look but the urns that Steve had waxed so poetic about were not there. What *was* there, hidden in the weeds, was a pair of handsome concrete urns molded in classical shapes. Steve apologized for not finding the urns he remembered, but would we be interested in the urns that were there? Of course, I said we would be pleased to have them and Nancy was delighted to make the donation.

Skinner delivered them to Tower Hill dropping them off at the north vestibule of the Stoddard building. They remained there for several years flanking a bench against the west wall until they were moved to the completed Limonaia in 2010.

The urns are entirely gray except for a distinct concave terracotta disc located just below the upper opening. Someone suggested that perhaps the pair was the work of Eric Ellis Soderholtz.

Soderholtz was a photographer and amateur gardener. He was fond of terracotta pots from Impruneta, Italy. "Impruneta" was the gold standard of terracotta garden ornaments. The terracotta is made from clay local to the area in Italy and has a red-colored finish. Unfortunately, the harsh winter weather in Maine where Soderholtz's garden was located proved devastating to his precious Italian pots. He took matters in hand and came up with the idea of casting concrete in the shapes of classical urns and garden pots. The results proved popular with serious gardeners but his simple cottage industry only lasted a few years.

Nancy Skinner had no memory of where her husband had acquired the pair so their provenance is lost. However, we were lucky to have them.

Several years later, I found myself on a tour at the home and garden of lifestyle *doyenne* Martha Stewart on Mt. Desert Island. Strategically decorating her garden were many Soderholtz ornaments. The tour included lunch which Martha herself served from behind a buffet table. When it was my turn to be served I broached the subject of her ornaments and let her know of the two urns at Tower Hill. Martha approached me as lunch concluded and asked if I would like to see a facsimile of the Soderholtz Catalog. Indeed I did. I followed her to the library (the house was once the summer home of Edsel Ford, coincidently also called Skylands) where we sat on a couch thumbing through the catalog until we found an image of the urns at Tower Hill. Martha's eyes grew wide and without hesitation she exclaimed, "I'll give you $10,000 for the pair."

With a smile and also without hesitation, I responded, "They were a gift in memory of a donor's husband and aren't for sale." Though she was disappointed, we continued to sit and companionably share the catalog. She assured me she would try to get a copy for the WCHS archive. We never got a copy.

The Last Acquisition

The last ornament I obtained for the Society was also from Nancy Skinner—ever a good friend to Tower Hill and me. For well over fifteen years I was aware of an ancient Roman sarcophagus sitting unattended in Nancy's Bolton garden. Steve Fletcher suggested I ask for it and I did. Nancy said, "No." She had plans for it to be a water feature in her yet-to-be-designed back garden. Steve told me to keep up the campaign to get the ornament to Tower Hill. So, for years I would jokingly mumble the word "sarcophagus" every time Nancy and I were together.

In late 2011, Nancy gave me a call and asked if we would like the Sarcophagus? Yes indeed. My idea was to display it in the Limonaia as a planter. It was "temporarily" put in the Library Garden, where, as of this writing, it still sits.

Roman sarcophagus, 2nd century, CE. Gift of Nancy Skinner

More times than I can remember, a phone call from the Boylston dispatcher would wake me in the night informing me to get "my ass" up to Tower Hill as quickly as possible and help the police or fire department deal with an issue in the Stoddard Center. I'd jump into my sweats and appropriate outer gear and meet them at the front door. It invariably had to do with the burglar alarm or the sprinkler systems. There was never a break-in or a fire. The building was just a bit too sensitive. It was fortunate that I lived a half mile distance from the front gate and was usually available to troubleshoot these occasional hiccups.

We had a string of good building superintendents but none better than Steve Smith from Holden. Steve was our first designated building director and the caretaker of the increasingly complex infrastructure that made Tower Hill work. By the time Steve joined our team the water system went as far as the Moss Steps in the Shade Garden and the Folly in the Inner Park. The electric power extended to the Barn, throughout the parking lots, the Lawn and Secret Gardens, and north to the far end of the Systematic Garden and Pliny's Fountain. The wiring was set up to accept the landscape lighting.

With my support, Steve kept a watchful eye on everything. He had a rapport with all vendors and tradespeople which was drawn from experience. He was a true Yankee; he spent the Society's money wisely. I made him promise not to retire before me. I couldn't bear the thought of having to replace him. But, he retired and I did. Steve Fluet started at Tower Hill a few weeks before I left in 2012.

It's always "easy" to build but hard to maintain. Maintenance is all-important. A new project should not be taken on if a maintenance plan is not in place.

Eventually the time came to repave Fuller Drive. The first paving laid in 1991 had withstood the construction traffic of three development phases, twenty winters, and a million-plus automobiles. It was wisely decided to wait until the Winter Garden and Limonaia were complete. Nine days and $130,000 later, the Drive was restored in mid-May. There was some worry that the substrata of the original road was compromised; it was not.

The last of the Phase IVA projects was to be the Container Court—later called the "Garden Within Reach"—a garden originally conceived for the physically challenged and their caregivers and also to educate people on garden accessibility.

The trustees entered into contract with Blair Hines for the design of the Container Court and Martha Pappas funded the schematic phase of the design. The area for the garden was relatively modest, the four boundaries being the Limonaia to the north, Farmhouse to the South, the granite curb and iron fence to the west, and the far end of the Farmhouse meeting room to the east. The one major existing detail to deal with was the 180-year-old white ash (*Fraxinus americana*), just southeast of the of the central doors of the Limonaia. We also instructed Blair to maintain the central path from the back door of the Farmhouse

John and Joann loving the ash, 2009

to the center door of the Limonaia—the last leg of the dramatic south to north axis.

Marillyn Zacharis was elected chairman of the Container Court Committee and Blair came up with an appropriate plan with an estimated price tag of $300,000. The primary goal of the garden was for it to be simple, displaying planters and containers that average gardeners, with varying degrees of disability, could recreate in their own gardens. We immediately went into action and started identifying funds for the construction of the garden. Encouraged by the Massachusetts Cultural Commission, we applied for capital funds specifically for the Container Court. We received word that the late Bob Courtemanche, Marillyn's dearest friend, had left a generous undisclosed bequest in support of the Container Court endowment.

Governor Deval Patrick and John at Tower Hill, November 2011. The Massachusetts Cultural Council awarded WCHS a grant of $89,000 for the development of the Container Court.

In early November, we were notified that the Massachusetts Cultural Commission awarded $89,000 for the garden. Massachusetts governor Deval Patrick chose Tower Hill as the location for his announcement of our award and several others. Construction was scheduled for spring of 2012. I retired before a shovel was put in the ground.

Blair's original plan for the Container Court was eventually replaced by a far more complicated and expensive plan by another design firm. It was completed and dedicated in 2016 at a cost of $1.5 million.

Interments

A few years before Bob Courtemanche died, we established an interment policy due to the large number of requests from members wanting to inter a loved one at Tower Hill. We associated an interment with the placement of a bench or the planting of a tree—a $10,000 or $5000 donation respectively. Bob's interment was under an umbrella-tree (*Magnolia tripetala*) off the Quarry Trail adjacent to the Folly. A few years earlier, Bob had placed a bench and a tree in memory of his son Richard off Tulip Tree Path. Many interments have occurred since, the favored spots being the Inner Park and the Shade Garden.

—⁂—

At the same time, the Society began to focus on ideas for the Children's Garden. Addressed on the Master Plan, the garden would be sited on the land between the Maintenance Barn and the south end of the parking lots. The concept was that it be a "farm" in miniature to reflect the agricultural heritage of Tower Hill with interactive features for children and parents—an idea the 1772 Foundation might embrace. A second area on the Master Plan that had "discovery potential" for families was the Wildlife Garden, an area bisected by the Loop Trail and the Old Farm Road to the south. It would have a cantilevered tree house for the viewing of the tree canopy, a bridge over a fern glen and a grotto for the observation of what occurs underground. Additional features would be determined by designer and an appointed committee.

NEWTON'S THIRD LAW

With so many ideas being tossed about, it became difficult to concentrate. What the idea makers failed to realize is that every idea would have a complex effect. Over the east door leading into the Limonaia, I had stenciled Newton's Third Law:

> TO EVERY ACTION, THERE IS ALWAYS
> AN EQUAL AND OPPOSITE REACTION

This can lead to "Mission Creep." It is all too common that well-meaning individuals lose sight of the goals of an institution. In spite of the clear and strong statement of purpose, supporting objectives and an intelligent Master Plan, Tower Hill is not immune.

—⚬⚬⚬—

My involvement in all of this came to an abrupt end in late November. My mother fell, broke her hip and died a week later. Bob and I had been my mother's primary caregivers since the early 2000s. We were not prepared for such an ending though she was ninety-three. The responsibility of arranging for her cremation and the realities of my own physical and emotional condition compelled me to start the process of retiring from the Society. My goal was to retire December of 2014 after finishing the Container Court and tying up loose ends for my successor—that was not to be. *C'est la vie.*

My last day as Executive Director of the Worcester County Horticultural Society and Founding Director of Tower Hill Botanic Garden was formally March 15, 2012—the Ides of March.

I am exceedingly grateful for my long tenure at WCHS. Few people are afforded the opportunity to create something so magnificent from scratch. I was rewarded many times for being in the right place at the right time—all of it possible because of the friendships made and the many supporters who connected to the vision of the Master Plan.

Emily and John, Christmas 2010

---------- Conclusion ----------

Festina Lente

CUPID WAS OFTEN up to mischief and no good came from the passion-instilling arrow that hit his nephew Pluto, god of the underworld, on one of his rare visits to the world of the sun. When Pluto laid eyes on his sister Ceres' daughter, his niece Proserpina, the arrow had its intended effect. There was no antidote and Destiny took control. He abducted the innocent girl and swiftly took her to the underworld where he made her his wife. Happy Pluto, unhappy Ceres, sniggering Cupid, dazed and confused Proserpina.

Pluto refused to return Proserpina to earth and Ceres plunged the earth into eternal winter—short, dark, cold days, no spring, no summer, no crops, no plants of any kind. Finally, a compromise was reached. Proserpina was permitted to live with her uncle/husband for six months, autumn and winter, and for six months with her mother, spring and summer.

This myth is a charming explanation of our six months of dormancy and six months of glorious growth and flower. As a gardener, I am acutely connected to and accepting of this seasonal compromise. I love

Above: Cedar of Lebanon (*Cedrus libani*)

the challenge of winter. It gives me the opportunity to think and wonder what I can do to outsmart the dull, dark dormancy. That long ago wish to understand the green, gray and brown that I saw passing as a blur through the car window—that wish came true. Now I know.

Just hours ago, Bob and I drove to and from the grocery store the day after Thanksgiving, a cold, damp and gloomy day. I was cheered however, by the shapes, textures, and colors of the Norway spruce, the white spruce, white pine, concolor fir, red cedar, and arborvitae, and also by the stark silhouettes of maple, oak, elm, beech, magnolia, dogwood and hickory. My bottomless desire to be seduced and embraced by plants sustains me. Like Proserpina I can bear and appreciate the subtle beauty of dormancy knowing what lies ahead in six months.

The delicious nature of currants, the spring bloom of sweet peas and lilacs, the evergreen dominance of southern magnolias, the unpleasant byproduct of gingko fruit, the genius of Vitruvian discipline in designing a garden—and knowing when to take a cookie when the cookies are passed—have served me well during my more than forty years in public horticulture. Lucky me.

Ah, but Tower Hill, what an interesting journey, from my awkward, less than professional, introduction to the Worcester County Horticultural Society in 1984 to a twenty-eight year love affair with its history and dynamic generous supporters. The rhythm and momentum of the four development phases, a completed project every five years—all happened without second-guessing or incurring debt. Although I was cast as a "benign dictator" in the dual role of visionary and taskmaster, the success of Tower Hill grew from a cadre of like-minded individuals who both understood the vision and supported it with generous resources and the sweat of their brows.

In 2014, Bob and I moved from our one-acre Maple Grove property in Boylston to a condo in a fifty-five and over development. I still feel like that weird little itinerant kid from California, fascinated by classical history and in awe of the natural world around me. Busts of Augustus and Hadrian have replaced Wagner and Liszt and I now garden intensively in a backyard of seven hundred square feet.

Festina Lente

Festina Lente, "Make Haste Slowly," has proven to be a strategic and philosophical guiding principle in the creation of a public garden and also in my journey through life. I thank the pantheon of spirits that give us—if we are open to it—the opportunities of knowing plants and all they provide us.

Statue of Cupid, given by Henry Ciborowski, atop its column near the Folly at Tower Hill

——— Appendx ———

Previous page: Black maple (*Acer saccharum* subsp. *nigrum*)

Ten Favorite Trees

1. Tulip tree (*Liriodendron tulipifera*) is a member of the Magnolia family, native to eastern North America as far north as southern Worcester County. It is the tallest growing native tree east of the Mississippi River, attaining a height of 190 feet. As a landscape tree it will grow 60 to 90 feet. This tree has had a grip on me since I first learned about it my sophomore year in college. Tom Buchter and I noticed a tree of great height growing in a thick forest on a west facing woodland well beyond the boundaries of the gardens at Skylands. We took a long hike into the woods and when we reached our goal, we identified the tree from its leaves as a tulip tree. This particular specimen had to have been well over 120 feet. From that day, I thought that if I could be reincarnated as anything, it would be a tulip tree. Knowing that Tower Hill was located in the northern most range of the species, I made it a goal to plant them in the Inner Park. The first one was in memory of Dr. Ann Nemitz and is located east of the Folly.

2. Bald cypress (*Taxodium distichum*) is a species I became familiar with at Skylands. It has one of the saddest stories of all trees on earth. It once was the dominant tree along the mid-Atlantic and southern coasts of North America. The wood is among the most durable and long-lasting in the world. When the southern states were colonized, the European settlers had no clue about the value of this tree. Instead of carefully harvesting the timber for export, they (their slaves) cut the trees, clearing the forests for rice fields. The coastline was destabilized, resulting in the obliteration of the rice fields during storm events. Rice continued to be cultivated until the end of the nineteenth century. The cypress does not naturally reforest itself and these great trees will never occur in the dominant way they once did. Several Taxodium have been planted in the

Meadow and Wildlife Garden at Tower Hill. They serve as a reminder of reckless human dominance over the natural world.

3. American chestnut (*Castanea dentate*) produces a wood of great durability and value like the bald cypress. It too was nearly clear-cut out of existence. At Tower Hill remnants of this tree can only be found north of Pliny's Allée. Though the tree was scarce, it still grew to great size and the delicious nuts were harvested in autumn. In 1904, a fungus was introduced to the east coast from Asia. It targeted the chestnut and devastated the few remaining natural plantations. A resistant variety is being sought.

4. American elm (*Ulmus americana*) has a spectacular winter silhouette. Though the wood has little use, the tree in its natural habitat stabilizes riverbanks and provides valuable shelter for a multitude of animals. Despite the fact it's native to moist soils, it does very well in dry urban landscapes which made it a popular street tree. It seems that every town in northeastern United States had an Elm Street. In 1928, a shipment of elm wood from the Netherlands was brought to Ohio. The wood contained beetles that transmitted a fungus fatal to the trees. By 1989 77 million elms had died, seventy-five percent of the population in the eastern United States. Many cities became treeless. There has been a concerted effort to find disease resistant cultivars. Several promising resistant forms have been planted at Tower Hill. Frank Harrington, Sr., initiated the planting with three Liberty elms in 1989, one in the meadow, two in the nursery, later moved to the parking lots.

5. Mountain silverbell (*Halesia monticola*), native to the southern Appalachian Mountains, is a forty-plus foot tree I became familiar with while working at Skylands in northern New Jersey. There was a large specimen in the azalea garden and also an impressive specimen terminating the view looking west to east on the Diana allée of Sargent cherries. It is grown purely for its showy white bell-like flowers that appear in May. The tree evoked such fond memories of my time at

Appendix

Skylands that I had one planted at the terminus of Pliny's Allée. As of this writing, it is where Bob and I intend to have our ashes placed.

6. Black gum (*Nyssa sylvatica*) is a native tree I like to call the "tinker toy tree" because of the arrangement of the branches at right angles to the trunk. It grows to about 50 feet in cultivation and up to 90 feet in the wild. It can be seen at Tower Hill on the perimeter of the vernal pool east of the Inner Park and there is also a specimen in the east border of the Lawn Garden. It has few to no insect or disease issues, has beautiful blue fruit attractive to birds and scarlet leaf color in the autumn. I became familiar with this species at Skylands where a fine specimen grew in the southwest border of the Moraine Garden. It is useful as a shade tree for both urban and suburban locations.

7. Juneberry (*Amelanchier x grandiflora* cv. 'Ballerina'). I've never met an Amelanchier I didn't like. I appreciate this one in particular because it was one of the first woody plants we installed at Tower Hill. It was a gift from Ernestine Blanchard in memory of her husband Russell who died in 1984. We planted the large shrub north of the lower end of Tower Hill Road. Amelanchiers are true harbingers of spring, blooming in April. There are a variety of species growing at Tower Hill. They all produce delicious pome fruit in early June. There are cultivated specimens in the Lawn Garden, Pliny's Allée, Inner Park, Flagpole Knoll, and Wildlife Garden.

8. Hiba cedar (*Thujopsis dolabrata* var. *hondai*). We received a Hiba cedar as a small slow-growing tree. We thought the leaf color complimented the siding of the Stoddard Center, so we planted it in the bed parallel to the southeast end of the building. In 2008, due to the expansion of the building, it had to be moved. We hired Bartlett Tree Service to do the job and were horrified when we watched them move it practically bare root to its new location southeast of parking lot #1. We held our breaths as the weeks ticked by to see if it would survive. Survive? It never stopped growing. This is no dwarf form; it's the real deal and

looks perfect as of this writing. It is at least twenty feet tall. A native of Japan where the wood is greatly valued, the tree has the potential to grow to ninety feet. A real prize.

9. Cedar of Lebanon (*Cedrus libani*) is native to Cyprus, the mountains of the Middle East and Turkey and is perfectly cold-hardy tree in Massachusetts. It is the national tree of Lebanon. The small specimen at Tower Hill that grows in the tree grove east of the Children's Garden was given by Richard Seder of North Grafton in memory of his father Leonard, a lawyer whose office was located near the Horticultural Building on Elm Street. The tree was planted as a symbol of hope for peace throughout the world. Richard hoped to see peace in the Middle East in his lifetime.

10. Black maple (*Acer saccharum* subspecies *nigrum*) is native to Massachusetts. I collected the specimens at Tower Hill, with permission, from watershed property in West Boylston. For a reason I can't explain, I've been mildly obsessed to find this tree in the wild. There is good reason to suspect that what I collected was a hybrid with the species. At any rate, my day was made when I found it during a hike on reservoir land. The specimen to the left of the entrance to the Lawn Garden is growing into a handsome tree. Its autumn color and the quality of its sap is equal to the species.

Appendix

PROPOSAL FOR THE NEW ENGLAND HORTICULTURAL CENTER

On February 2, 1983, trustees Paul Rogers and Alden Miller offered their ideas on what a horticulture center should encompass.

—⚘—

The main reason for the existence of the New England Horticultural Center (NEHC) would be to interface people with plants using as many dimensional experiences as will further this goal.

It will strive to inform the public, both general and professional, as to the proper identification, display, and culture of plant material. This will be done by the sensitive development and proper maintenance of display plantings. An attempt will be made to use a wide variety of plants in aesthetically pleasing and informative arrangements so as to give maximum visual impact.

It will be necessary to develop and maintain supportive facilities for equipment and materials storage, a greenhouse complex, an extensive library for staff and public, and lecture and teaching facilities.

It would seem advisable to set up a Board of Directors for the NEHC as soon as the potential for a Center moves toward actuality. It would seem that WCHS is the sponsoring agency but to insure continuity, the Bd. of Dir. NEHC and its advisory groups should be separate from WCHS. There is a need for, and many advantages to, forming an extended advisory group that would be composed of representatives from professional, para-professional, and lay groups. Liaison with the Extension Services, shade and forestry laboratories, professional organizations, plant societies, horticultural institutions, and the commercial sector would provide NEHC with technical information, at the same time as it broadens our up-to-date knowledge base.

There is a need, ASAP, of a financial group for NEHC. It will be necessary to co-develop the physical form (grounds & buildings) at the same time as a major fund raising activity is carried on to provide for the initial physical development of the Center. It may be assumed that after five to seven years admission fees and membership will carry an ever-increasing percentage of the annual budget, but an endowment fund in excess of two million dollars will be necessary from the very early stages to assure that a base level of activity can be scheduled at least two years in advance.

I believe very strongly that to provide the vision necessary for the correct physical planning of NEHC to take place, a landscape development concern will be needed. To assure an orderly, logical, consistent development of the entire physical property, it will be necessary to have a master plan for grounds development, parking, utilities, and buildings. The specific location of the main building complex will determine most other aspects of the grounds lay-out. Thus, this location must be decided at an early stage.

Only a landscape architectural firm would have the training to properly arrange the buildings and land for maximum and logical effect. The LA would work within the framework provided by the NEHC Bd. of Dir. For example, they would need to know in general and somewhat specifically what was wanted e.g., no major change in land forms, two or more ponds, parking for xx cars with expansion built in for x + y cars, that the layout is primarily for visual effect, that they would work for a specific fee not a percentage of the development costs, etc., etc.

Building(s) would need to be sensitive to New England (not an ego trip for the designer), be energy efficient, have a percentage of movable or adaptable interior spaces to adjust to changing needs, be capable of expansion, and units that we can be proud of and live with. Perhaps, the buildings are a project that belongs totally separate from the land planning section.

All is subject to much discussion, adjustment, and revision.

Trust that it will serve as a springboard for dialogue. Hope it helps.

Sincerely,
Paul Rogers, (Alden Miller)

Appendix

From the Tower Hill Working Paper, January 14, 1987

Before beginning the physical plan of the gardens, Environmental Planning and Design created a "Working Paper" in 1987 to serve as the basis of the Tower Hill Master Plan. The paper provided a preliminary analysis of the site and the regional context of Tower Hill and went on to present a distillation of the Society's goals for a Horticultural Center. The following are excerpts from this portion of the document dealing with three primary program components of a botanic garden: research, education, and displays and collections. Also included are excerpts from the preliminary building program.

The Working Paper remains a valuable resource for the history of Tower Hill's development and is available for review in the library.

Research

True botanical gardens have three major program components: research, education, and displays and collections. The first component separates a botanic garden from a display garden. Research programs can be botanical, involving plant research on the molecular level, plant exploration, and plant taxonomy. This means botanists on staff and lab space for their projects. Most university-related programs are headed in this direction. It is not in Tower Hill's plans to provide any facilities for this kind of research themselves, but rather to cooperate with any existing university programs as they request it. Any research program at Tower Hill will be horticultural in nature involving plant testing and trials. While there is no desire to establish such a program at the outset, planning should not preclude it in the future. Over the long term this kind of program will require nursery space, which does not have to be on the site. It will also require a staff person to run the trials, do the evaluations, and publish the results. Other than office space, this type of research program would not require any special space in a building.

Education

The educational programs at botanical gardens have become more and more important over time as institutions begin to look for outside funding and have to justify their role in the community. Education is the major means to bring the gardens and collections alive and develop a loyal and enthusiastic following. The development of such a program has implications for staffing, for building requirements, and for the layout of the gardens themselves. The main groups that Tower Hill looks to serve are visitors, adults, elementary school groups, and professionals.

For the visitor to get the maximum benefit out of the facilities at Tower Hill, they must be well interpreted, signed, and labelled. But probably the best way to interpret the displays is to offer guided tours. It is that personal touch that brings the topic alive, openly transmits enthusiasm, and promotes give and take so questions can be answered on the spot. There must be places in the gardens for groups to gather and listen. Guiding tours is an area where volunteers can contribute enormously to the success of the Garden, and it is for this benefit alone that Tower Hill might consider instituting a volunteer program. A volunteer coordinator will be required with corresponding office space.

The adult education program will consist of classes, lectures, and special programs and shows as it does currently. By catering to this group the Garden can build a strong base of support. Tower Hill will return to putting on the smaller shows that they used to have in Botany Hall when an appropriate space is available. There are no plans to return the Spring Show to the Centrum in downtown Worcester. It would be held on Horticultural Society grounds. It will be desirable to develop a children's education program in conjunction with the schools, but the impetus would probably have to come from the Garden since the schools do not have the money to institute such a program. Teachers will continue to be drawn from the community and the staff as required.

The final element in the educational program is the library. The existing collection is 7000 volumes, one half of which are from the nineteenth century. The library will also contain the herbarium which

Appendix

will be very small and will only serve to bolster the plant collection. There will be a full-time librarian.

The space requirements for the educational program are for four offices plus secretarial space and storage. The library will consist of the regular stacks, a rare book room, and an office. Classes and shows would be held in a large multi-purpose space that could be subdivided according to need into three classrooms for thirty each or meeting rooms. In conjunction with this space there must also be a workshop/set-up space, and storage for tables and chairs. Space for expansion should be provided.

DISPLAYS

The site at Tower Hill is very assertive. There are the long views to the Wachusett Reservoir, the hills, the rock pushing to the surface, and the extensive but fragile wetlands. The challenge to the institution is to develop a unique program sensitive to the site that works with it and enhances and uses its positive features. Normally separate garden elements may well be integrated into new combinations. The focus of the garden must be suburban and rural rather than urban to match the needs of the Garden's constituency. But above all the Garden must be a beautiful place with each space flowing gently into the next in the best tradition of estate gardening.

Tower Hill will evaluate all plants that are added to the collections as to their economic, ornamental, and ecological value. There will not be any attempt to show a representation of all the plants that can be grown in the Central Massachusetts area. This policy does not preclude the development of comprehensive collections so long as they meet the criteria stated above.

After distilling the comments of the staff and the Master Planning Committee the following displays have emerged as the preliminary program for Tower Hill.

There is the recognition that given the long New England winter there will be the need to extend the garden season with a CONSERVATORY development. There is the desire here to look back to the orangerie for inspiration rather the Victorian tropical house, to "combine eighteenth century elegance with twentieth century technology" to create a more energy efficient space for growing plants. Major glass areas would be oriented ideally to the southeast through southwest while the north side would have no glass at all. The roof does not necessarily have to be all glass. The conservatory development needs to be phased, so the design must be broken into different houses that can be built incrementally. The initial orangerie would be about 4000 SF, and it has been suggested that space might be reserved on the site to add other units up to about 15,000 SF total. It is our experience that a critical mass of display must be reached to attract visitors to a site. The greenhouse area is actually quite small here, if it were compared to the 22,000 SF in the East Conservatory at Longwood. However, the effect of the house at Longwood is relatively less for its size because the total house can be grasped immediately upon entering, and the display is massed rather than meted out as one winds through the space. But because we are not convinced that 15,000 SF, no matter how carefully configured, will approach the required critical mass of display, we would recommend that additional space be reserved on the site for more conservatory buildings.

The display that has been discussed for this space is one that will expand by example the palette of materials that people grow in their homes. The plants will be scaled to the space though and not just to the typical home. The emphasis will be on display and bloom and fragrance rather than typical low light tropicals. Such winter blooming plants as camellias, begonias, and forced bulbs would be interspersed with fragrant jasmines and lemon trees. The orangerie should be situated in a way to be visible from an adjacent space that can accommodate dinner parties or an afternoon chamber concert. In the summer the conservatories should open directly onto terraces where one might sit and still hear the gentle sounds of water inside. It is also our experience that people love to see things they cannot grow themselves, like orchids and carnivorous plants and forced spring flowers, and that some of the expansion space should be set aside to show some of these things. Close

Appendix

to the center of things there is need for a GREAT LAWN surrounded by planting of choice trees and evergreens that serve as a framework for masses of flowering shrubs, naturalized bulbs including lilies, and unusual groundcovers. The lawn could be set up for an afternoon croquet match or covered with a tent for parties or perhaps weddings.

There are several displays that serve to draw people into the garden. One of these is a FLOWER GARDEN. This garden might integrate bulbs and annuals into the traditional perennial borders for a burst of color from early spring through frost. Even the smaller flowering shrubs could be incorporated as they are in English gardens. Flowers might be grouped for color, for fragrance, for suitability for cutting, or for ease of maintenance to increase the educational value of the display.

There has been interest expressed in having a ROSE GARDEN. Instead of the traditional hybrid teas, this garden might select new and old roses not only for their beauty in flower but also for their attractiveness as a whole plant and for their disease resistance, hardiness, and fragrance. The whole display might be planned for fragrance, and other plants included to extend the bloom and show roses integrated into the rest of the garden rather than rigidly confined to their own formal beds.

Another major display would be the FRUIT AND VEGETABLE GARDEN, since this of great interest to a lot of people in the area. The fruit area would include not only all kinds of fruit trees, but also small fruits such as strawberries, raspberries, grapes and blueberries. There would also be nut trees and unusual fruits such as kiwi, quince, and persimmon. Such techniques as espaliers, cordons, pruning grape vines, and growing a fruit tree hedge could be demonstrated. The vegetable gardens might contain exhibits on intensive growing techniques, growing vegetables in containers, new vegetables selected for disease resistance and flavor, vegetables from other cultures, and how to integrate vegetables into the ornamental garden. This garden area might also contain the herb garden within it as an ornamental feature.

Also in association with this garden there would be the S. LATHROP DAVENPORT PRESERVATION ORCHARD of old apple varieties. This is an historic collection at the Worcester County Horticultural

Society—some 230 trees presently. They are on M-7 semi-dwarf stock, and would require an area of about three and a half to four acres.

There was some discussion of the possibilities of having a garden of botany for doctors or a witches garden. These are all aspects of the same topic, the chemurgic uses of plants. It was the possibility of finding new medicinal plants and spices that spurred much of the early exploration. The origins of the modern botanic garden can be found in the early physic gardens that were established. It is only within fairly recent times that plants have been collected solely for their ornamental qualities. Perhaps Tower Hill might develop a modern PHYSIC GARDEN that looks to the past to the origins of botanic gardens and to the historic past of New England with plants of the Indians and the early settlers. But it would also look to the present and to the future for the use of plants in medicine and in industry.

A HOME DEMONSTRATION GARDEN is overtly geared to educating the public about plants and horticulture. It can address all aspects of the home garden such as the best plants for a given situation such as gardening on a bank or gardening in the shade; the best hedge materials or groundcovers or whatever for the Central Massachusetts area; shrub or flower borders for early spring bloom; growing plants in containers; and special gardening ideas for the handicapped. These gardens can be flexible and exhibits can be changed over time to address new gardening problems.

Several garden developments are related to particular environmental areas. One such development would be the ROCK GARDEN which would be located on one of the areas with existing rock outcrops. It might consist of all plants including trees, shrubs, perennials, and lichens that thrive under these conditions, not just the traditional alpines. It might contain shady areas as well as sunny so that it truly is a rock garden for Central Massachusetts. A special collection for including in this area might be the dwarf conifers.

There are extensive areas of wetland on the eastern edges of the site. Though their development potential is severely restricted by the state in the Wetland Protection Act, they can be developed as WETLAND

Appendix

or WATER GARDENS with care. It might be possible to develop a wildlife pond of three to four acres down in the valley or even a series of smaller ponds, but this will require further investigation by an engineer. This would provide the habitat for growing water and water edge plants such as hardy water lilies, and drifts of water iris and arrowhead punctuated by bold clumps of umbrella plant. A woodland stream garden might have large areas of ferns, lobelia, primroses and astilbe clumped around small pools. Finally boardwalks might wind their way through boggy areas planted with clumps of the native deciduous hollies and swamp azaleas and patches of skunk cabbage and marsh marigolds as well as non-native ornamentals that thrive in these conditions.

A major display would be THE SHADE OR WOODLAND GARDEN. This garden should cover several different environmental conditions from damp low areas to dry upland areas. It would contain all ornamental plants, native and non-native, that grow in shaded conditions. The forest floor might be carpeted with drifts of ferns, hosta, and spring bulbs all framed by massings of flowering shrubs and small flowering trees such as witch hazel and dogwood. A major component of this garden would be the ericaceous plants—rhododendrons, azaleas, and mountain laurel. It has been suggested that a good part of the show from this collection might be massed along the entry drive into the site.

Finally a WILDLIFE GARDEN would be developed to show how to provide wildlife habitat and food in an attractive landscape setting. The emphasis here would be on ornamentals to attract birds especially. There might also be a small fish pond as a focus to this garden.

The remainder of the site would be developed with NATURE TRAILS through the meadows and woods and threaded through the wetlands on boardwalks. The object would be to group native plants in the proper associations for each environmental area along the trail. The existing vegetation would be supplemented and enhanced for the purposes of improving the educational value of the relatively small area available in the Garden. There is no desire to compete with the existing nature programs and preserves in the area, but rather to complement their efforts, and provide another botanical experience on the site.

Administration

The requirements for administrative space will grow as Tower Hill continues to grow. Six offices for the director, administrative assistant, horticulturist, director of development, membership secretary, and one additional will be required. Additionally, there will be space required for secretaries, a copying/workroom, restrooms, and storage. Room for expansion should be provided.

Maintenance and Production

The complete program for the maintenance facilities would include the following: vehicular storage of four bays plus one work bay; a workshop; employee facilities including restrooms, showers, lockers, and a lunch room; a superintendent's office; tool storage; locked, heated chemical storage; regular storage; outside bins for mulch, compost, and other supplies; and leaf storage. Major mechanical work will no be done on the premises.

The conservatories will require back-up greenhouse space both for the permanent displays and for the seasonal plants. The most convenient location for these facilities would be to be connected to the conservatories themselves.

Poly houses will be adequate for the Garden's use. The current plan is to have the annuals for the outdoor displays contract grown, though much of it could probably be fit into the production facilities as outlined. In addition there would need to be a head house for potting, cold frames, storage, and a lath house. This area should also have room for expansion.

Finally, a two to three acre nursery will be required. Its location is very flexible.

Appendix

Visitors Center

Spaces specially allocated to visitor services will be needed increasingly as Tower Hill grows. A visitors center would contain not only restrooms, but also an orientation area with a reception desk where advice on what to see, maps, and other information would be dispensed. This would also be the place where a fee could be collected. The orientation space could also function as an exhibit space.

There are plans to have a gift shop at Tower Hill, and it might be another thing that the volunteers could do. The gift shop will require substantial storage. A restaurant would be a highly desirable feature at Tower Hill, since there are not currently any good places near the Garden to find lunch or a snack. A restaurant would have an outdoor dining terrace associated with it. Most profitable restaurant operations currently existing in gardens are leased to outside concerns who also do all the catering for special events and parties in the gardens. It will require further investigation to determine whether a restaurant facility at Tower Hill will be feasible given our projected numbers of visitors. Ideally both the restaurant and the gift shop would be accessible to visitors before they pay the entrance fee.

The two final facilities required in a visitors center are a members' room and a volunteers' room. The volunteers should have a place they can assemble, store their belongings, and socialize. The members' room also could be used for important meetings and functions.

PRELIMINARY BUILDING PROGRAM – VISITORS CENTER PHASE ONE

1. Multi-purpose space   3000 sf
   exhibit, shows, meeting, classrooms (3)
2. Workshop/set up   1000 sf
3. Storage   200 sf
   tables and chairs
4. Gift shop   2000 sf
   including storage

5.	Orangerie	4000 sf
6.	Restaurant dining room and kitchen	2250 sf
7.	Restrooms	750 sf
8.	Reception	2400 sf
9.	Library stacks, rare book room, office	2400 sf
10.	Offices five plus secretarial space and storage	800 sf
11.	Members room	900 sf
12.	Volunteers room	250 sf
13.	Mechanical/circulation	4550 sf
Total		24,500 sf

The additional 11,000 square feet of conservatory space belongs in future phases.

Circulation

Vehicular circulation through the site will be restricted to maintenance and emergency vehicles. All garden spaces should be accessible to a pick-up. Visitor access to the site will be through a single entrance off of French Drive and up through the site to the parking area and visitors center. From there access will be on foot or perhaps by tram. All gardens, though not necessarily all paths within them, must be handicapped accessible. Because of the extremes of topography on this site, it may well be that the only way to provide adequate handicapped access is with a tram.

Parking

Total parking requirements fluctuate widely depending on the day of the week and the time of the year. Gardens experience peak loading on their parking on Sunday afternoons in May and June. It is impractical

Appendix

to provide parking to handle these few Sundays. Initially, because there are relatively few things to see on the site, visits will be brief, and there will be a high turnover in the parking area increasing its capacity. As Tower Hill approaches 150,000 visitors and the Garden develops there will be a need for about 200 cars with about 100 spaces available as grass overflow. Additionally there must be some provision for bus parking and for future expansion.

Jay Hill, President of the Massachusetts Horticultural Society, presents the Society's Gold Medal to John, 1992

Appendix

Awards and Prizes

During my tenure and after, I was honored to receive the following awards and prizes for my accomplishments at Tower Hill Botanic Garden. Though presented to me, they are a credit to the Worcester County Horticultural Society's focus on the development of Tower Hill.

Gold Medal of the Massachusetts Horticultural Society, 1992, 1997

Garden Club of America, The Mrs. Oakleigh Thorne Medal, 2000

Rhode Island Spring Flower Show, Allen C. Haskell Lifetime Achievement in Horticulture Award, February 2001

National Garden Club Award of Excellence, 2009

Massachusetts Senate official citation for 25 years of service, 2009

Massachusetts House of Representatives official citation for 25 years of service, 2009

Worcester Telegram and Gazette Community Vision Award, 2009

Massachusetts Senate official citation for cultural enrichment, 2010

United States Senate official recognition, March 2012

Massachusetts Horticultural Society George Robert White Medal of Honor, 2012

Horticulture Club of Boston Award of Recognition for the development of Tower Hill Botanic Garden, December 2013

ACKNOWLEDGMENTS

SHORTLY AFTER BOB AND I moved to our condo at Park Place in Westborough, I discovered—down-slope from where I was making a garden—a wetland complete with flowing spring. I cut an opening in the secondary woods edging the wetland in order to have access to the area surrounding the spring. When it was suitably cleaned up, I began adding woody and herbaceous plants that should be growing there but had not yet been introduced by the slow cadence of natural succession.

During this time of discovery, I happily identified an American linden (*Tilia americana*). It grows to the left of the opening as you enter the wetland and keeps company with a healthy female winterberry holly (*Ilex verticillata*). To the right stands an oak that I have yet to identify—two healthy young trees flanking the opening to my little bit of indigenous paradise.

During the summer of 2016, while driving long distances, I listened to Ovid's *Metamorphoses*. The book is a collection of myths and stories from the classical period. One story is about a husband and wife named Philemon and Baucis who showed such kindness to Jupiter and Mercury, that the gods promised to grant them any wish. All they wanted was, when the time came for them to die, they would die together. One living without the other was incomprehensible. Jupiter agreed to grant them their wish. When their time came after many long and happy years, Jupiter turned the soul of Baucis into a linden tree and the soul of Philemon into an oak tree.

John and Bob, 2017
Photo by Tony King

Acknowledgments

NONE OF THIS could have happened without the support of hundreds of friends and supporters.

Thanks must go to: Robert Zeleniak for being a supportive partner and the person that keeps me standing on two feet, Ingrid Mach and Jock Herron of TidePool Press for encouraging me to write this book and designing, editing and publishing it with such care and attention to detail, Kathy Bell for sharing the riches of the WCHS Library, Isabel Arms who saw right through me and supported me along my wonderful WCHS journey, Paul Rogers for getting the ball rolling, Fred Roberts for his early support, Elizabeth Scholtz and Charlie Mazza for talking across me, Marjorie Lodding who always told you what you needed to know, Henry Ciborowski and family for their love of beautiful gardens, Lee Charrier for her creative tenacity, Pete Moss for her lifetime of garden wisdom, Helen Stoddard for her belief in me from the get-go, Phil Beals for excelling as President, Hope and Ivan Spear for many surprises, Dick Dearborn for maintaining an even keel, Sid and Frank Callahan for understanding the romantic nature of gardens, Laura Callahan for her talents and energy, Julia Agrippina for displaying the power and determination of an immortal empress, Gale and Flip Morgan for their thirty plus years of friendship and their support of the Master Plan, Kitty Ferguson for loving Tower Hill, Louise Riemer for good conversation, Roger and Elizabeth Swain for their humor and encouragement, Chloe Sundberg for her patronage, Ken Hedenburg for the eternal love he had for Jeanette, Tom O'Connell who could see the world inside out, Nat Dexter who understood the role of a trustee, Ken Druse for his artistry, prose and humor, Deedee Burnside for her love of nature, superb calligraphy and, with Judy Cinquina, helping me start the New Jersey Native Plant Society, Marco Polo Stufano for sharing his genius for color, texture and display, Margaret Roach for selfless support, Barbara Booth for her understanding and support, John and Marianne Jeppson for their patronage, Blair Hines for helping put the puzzle together, Leonard Sophrin for his love of steel, Nancy Grimes and Humphrey Sutton for their generosity and setting an ornamental tone, Henry Rudio for starting the process of modernization, Scott Ewing for his conservative eye, Mary Ann and Frank Streeter for sharing their family's legacy of gardening excellence, Peter and Shirley Williams for their love of stone, Tay Ann Jay for being a romantic, Arthur and Martha Pappas who liked Tower Hill, Dr. Katherine Upchurch and Dr. Mark Schlickman for keeping me in one piece, Jesse and Dan Farber for sharing their talents, Karen Perkins for her hard work and friendship, Paul and Judy Trudeau for supporting the long history of Spring Flower Shows, Jeremy O'Connell for being my first guide in Rome, Mezitt Family and Bigelow Family for their generosity and love of great plants, Marillyn Zacharis for her friendship and support, Robert Courtemanche for his soul, Judy and Tony King and Val and Steve Loring for supporting their mother's love of Tower Hill and for being treasured confidants and friends, Worcester Garden Club for its support, Russ and Joyce Fuller for living across the street and understanding the value of a public garden, Tony Tilton and Warner Fletcher for lending their ears and supporting the garden, Jim French for his love of open space, Chet Kulisa for his love of soil, Susan Dumaine for her intelligence, Jim Tiemeyer for his riddle, Linda Milton for helping to lead the march, Cacky Hodgson for her thoughtfulness, Clayton Fuller for being the human divining rod, Martha Bigelow for understanding the importance of endowment, Steve Fletcher for his humor and salesmanship, Nancy Skinner for sharing her treasures, Joann Vieira for being tireless, Mike Arnum for understanding the onus, Arthur Lupien for introducing us to Ed Cary, Peter Oberdorf for legal council, Tom Buchter for starting me on the road of public service, Hans and Miek Bussink for feeding me and sharing their love of music, Harold Epstein, Tom Everett, Stuart Longmuir and Ben Blackburn for their memories of Clarence McKenzie Lewis, Russell Myers for teaching me diplomacy, Kathy Pitney for consistent support, Tom Mountain for his inspiration, Ginger Blais and all the Trail Blazers for battling invasive plants, Jack Craig and Manabu Saito for friendship, Frank Cabot and Tom Armstrong for their support, Rosemary Verey and Christopher Lloyd for adding credibility to the Tower Hill project, Rosemary Monahan and Stefan Cover for loving magnolias and planting a collection in the

Acknowledgments

Inner Park and for being great friends, Phyllis Stoddard for all her talents, John Stoddard for being one of my first friends in Worcester and my first audience as Director, George Bernardin for his humor, John Mirick for keeping me out of trouble, Isabel Lane and Maureen Pedroli for being the queens of hors d'oeuvre and Emily Munroe Hutchison and Burton Robert Trexler, my mother and father, who encouraged my interest in gardening.

I apologize to the many I have left out. Remember, this is all based on a fading memory.

Blood in the Veins

The successful realization of the Tower Hill Master Plan was due to many donors making significant contributions towards the four phases and also the hundreds of volunteers who supported all facets of the

A group of the many volunteers that support Tower Hill. Ann Marie Pilch, Education Director, is standing second row, far left.

operation. Whether they were stuffing envelopes, folding newsletters, manning the phones, parking cars, making the Plant Sale possible, pulling weeds, deadheading daylilies, pruning in the orchard, touring visitors, popping corn, making hors d'oeuvre, manning the reception desk, hanging pictures in the gallery, selling memberships, eradicating invasive plants, painting props for flower shows, working the cash registers, helping the librarian, scanning slides, overseeing classes, and the gods know much more, the volunteers are the life's blood of WCHS.

I absolutely—positively—should not single anyone out but there are a few that are conspicuous by frequent attendance and/or their varied talents. First and foremost is Frank Bisset. Frank accomplished many of the tasks listed above—always with a smile and an even disposition—working smoothly alongside staff. Judy Bisset supported the mezzanine staff on a regular basis. Natalie Perkins, who as of this writing is one hundred years old, and Mary O'Connor appeared every Monday to man the reception desk. Ginger Blais, Bob Pezzini and Pete Chadwick worked with me for years as we cleared trails and removed invasive plants. Barbara Pezzini supported Joann Vieira with the ever-important Plant Records. Bonny O'Brien, Betty Berry, and Roberta Pospisil have been integral to the library doing a myriad of projects.

To all of them, and the ones I've neglected to mention, thank you.